Love
Remains

Love Remains, A Guide Through Grief Copyright 2021 © Tracy Stone

Published and printed by Ignite Publishing a division of JBO Global Inc.
5569-47th Street Red Deer, AB
Canada, T4N1S1 1-877-677-6115

Cover design by Dania Zafar
Book design by Dania Zafar and JB Owen
Designed in the United States of America, Printed in China
ISBN: 978-1-7923-4179-3
First edition: December 2021

Ordering Information: Quantity sales. Special discounts are available on quantity purchases by corporations, associations, and others. For details, contact the publisher at the above address. Programs, products, or services provided by the author are found by contacting them directly. Resources named in the book are found in the resources pages at the back of the book.

Author Details: Tracy Stone - available at https://limitlesspotential.co.uk/love-remains.

Aladdin™ is a registered trademark of Disney Enterprises, Inc.
Bovril™ is a registered trademark of Unilever Supply Chain, Inc.
Chanel No. 5™ is a trademark of Chanel, Inc.
Dennys™ is a registered trademark of Duffy Meats Limited
DeLorean™ is a registered trademark of DeLorean Motor Company
Fahrenheit™ is a registered trademark of Parfums Christian Dior.
Indiana Jones™ is a registered trademark of Lucasfilm Ltd. LLC,
Magnum™ is a registered trademark of Conopco, Inc.
Matrix™is a registered trademark of Warner Bros. Entertainment Inc.
Perspex™ is a registered trademark of Perspex International Limited.
Rolls Royce™ is a registered trademark of Rolls-Royce Motor Cars Limited.
Turkish Delight™ is a registered trademark of Cadbury UK Limited
Urban Dictionary™ is a registered trademark of Urban Dictionary, LLC.
Whac-A-Mole™ is a registered trademark of Mattel, Inc.
YouTube™ is a registered trademark of Google LLC.
7-Up™ is a registered trademark of Dr Pepper/Seven Up, Inc.

Love
Remains

A Guide Through Grief

TRACY STONE

PREVIOUS BOOKS

Ignite Happiness

Ignite Possibilities

DEDICATION

For HGLD,

Who taught me to never borrow tractors.

My infinite gratitude, love, and admiration go to Mum, Gina, and Ciara, my three living angels, and to Simon for your love, support, guidance, patience, understanding, and countless cups of tea.

Sincere thanks also to Esther, Pat, and Charlene for your generosity and willingness to share your deeply personal experiences, perspective, and wisdom with me. You have added depth, color, heart, and soul to these pages.

TESTIMONIALS

As one of my original Rapid Transformational Therapy training alumni, I'm proud to see how Tracy has used the RTT skills that she gained, powerfully incorporating its transformative elements into her book *Love Remains*. In it, Tracy has created a book that is emotional, connecting, and beautifully written. She has created a place for those who are grieving to explore, understand, and evolve their journey through grief. This book is full of insightful learnings and resilience-building easy-to-do action steps. The exercises in every chapter enable the reader to personalize the book and their experience of grief, and to find comfort and resilience, while coming to terms with their grief. I am delighted to see the impact of the therapy that Tracy weaves through the pages, much of which has been embraced through her RTT training with me. I know that this book can make a difference in the lives of those who have lost someone special.

Marisa Peer, Best-selling author, world renowned speaker, creator of Rapid Transformational TherapyTM and the I am Enough movement

This book is a collection of tender moments, loving suggestions, and the move-the-needle-on-your-grief kind of support that goes beyond what other books in this genre do. Tracy Stone infuses her own 'heartfelt' grieving process to help you overcome your own. She laces her book with love and adoring antidotes that will help you come through your own loss stronger, braver, and remembering the love that so poignantly remains.

JB Owen, CEO and Founder of Ignite Publishing and JBO Global Inc. Speaker, Philanthropist, and 18 time International Best-Selling Author

Every person who has lost a loved one should read this. The book wraps you in a hug, helps you remember the love you shared, then gently inches you forward into living again. It holds your hand and only lets go when you're ready. The strategies Tracy shares are practical, heartwarming, and fun.

Alex Blake, International Best Selling Author and Editor, Brisbane, Australia

Love Remains is a gift to anyone grieving a deep loss. As someone who connects with the pain of losing a father, I identified with and absorbed every gut-wrenching, heart-rending detail poured out on the pages. Tracy has an amazing way of vividly sharing her vulnerability around her greatest loss, while also creating powerful and uplifting self-help techniques she calls "Baby Steps." These techniques not only provide a clear framework for healing, but also acknowledge that your grief journey is uniquely unfolding as it rightfully should be for you. If you are in the midst of grieving an unbearable loss, pick up this book to know you are not alone, and there is a path for moving forward.

Cindy Tank-Murphy, fellow grieving daughter and survivor of suicide loss

Tracy's book is written with so much love and compassion. I haven't had a lot of grief in my life yet, but I know that I will have a tremendous tool at my disposal when it happens. She openly depicted her own story, which allowed us to receive her advice with ease. Her powerful insights felt like a breeze that envelops your heart at times when the ground of life is shaken. I could easily relate with grief when I had a heartbreak with my ex-fiancée, and I know the "advice to my current-day self" exercise would have been instrumental in my healing. I am so grateful that Tracy took the time to give the readers great practical tools to help us return to the beautiful state of self-love and gratitude for life.

Francis Piché, Resilience Mindset Coach, Keynote Speaker, Founder and CEO of Resilience Element, https://www.francispiche.com/

Tracy's experiences and approaches to grief are a breath of fresh air. Not only does she provide you with interactive exercises and positive ways to deal with your grief, but she does so in a proactive way, helping you to emerge from the tunnel of grief as a stronger person. Tracy's sincere storytelling and amazing guidance are amazing examples of how to make the most of a challenging situation. Thanks for sharing, Tracy!

Chloe Holewinski, Translator and Editor

When I opened *Love Remains* by Tracy Stone, I was met with a warm feeling of empathy from the author. I felt as though I was with her in person, as she invited me to "make a comforting drink and sit with me for a while." It was like she was there in real life, and her words were so calm and thoughtful that she is someone, you know, who would share, listen, and give comfort. The book carried on in this vein, one of love and support. Throughout the book, I felt as though I was being hugged and no longer alone with any feelings of sadness that might have evoked from reading on. The book does have its laugh-out-loud moments, especially when Tracy mentions putting on 'big girl pants' and getting on with things. The book is relatable, and the reader feels an instant connection with the words on the page. It is easy to read, while still being filled with beautiful and insightful language which makes you think, "I am okay, this is okay. This is all part of life." Thank you for writing this book Tracy, the world needed your fresh and honest approach.

Tara Aisha, Head of Drama, Therapist, Author

Heartfelt and emotional, yet practical and supportive, I found the personal conversations with the reader in this book helpful and enlightening. At a time when one's thoughts are scattered, as if fired from a gun, the exercises helped me to focus on the best of times, while still encouraging me that life does go on and we should still follow our hearts.

Louise Searle, Somerset, UK

This is a beautifully written book, as the author gives an incredible, heartwarming tribute to her late father. Her magnificent story brought me to tears as she skillfully brought me front and center into her world of love, grief, and empowerment.

Curtis Ghee, Speaker and Best-selling Author

Love Remains is a refreshing, thoughtful, and tender perspective on grief. Tracy shares her own intimate journey with grief, and gives her readers permission to have their own unique experience with their grief while being held in nurturance and support through her "Baby Steps." During moments of this book, time stood still as I found myself in a deeply shared and understood experience of my own recent grief. Although this is a must-read book for anyone navigating the messy reality of grief, the truth is that, through all the "Baby Steps," the reader will receive powerful coaching as a guideline for life.

Diana Lockett, M.Sc., Canada's ONLY Re-Alignment Coach, You can Re-Align to Thrive™, www.dianalockett.com

This book takes you by the hand and leads you on a journey through the wilderness of grief. With her exquisite and deeply touching words, Tracy courageously unveils what a privilege it is to feel the pain of loss when we love so immensely. I shed many tears while reading *Love Remains*, and know it will be a valuable resource and literary hug to many who have lost someone close. It is a reminder that when we open ourselves to the fragility of life, we can bathe in the precious gift of what it truly means to be alive. Thank you, Tracy, and thanks to your Dad for leaving this generous legacy.

Sarah Cross, New Zealand

Love Remains is a stunningly beautiful compendium of deep insights, heartfelt strategies, and gracefully magical recipes that are strung together by a golden thread of wisdom, guiding you every step of the way along your very own uniquely different journey through grief. I've experienced a lot of it over the last five years, mostly due to cancer; I wish I'd had this book then to guide me through the tumultuous twists and turns that grief took me through. Tracy Stone shares her stories with such brilliance, depth, and presence, I'd highly recommend *Love Remains* to anyone facing this journey, which at some point in time, we all do. Thank you, Tracy!

Amy Hackett-Jones, Peace Whisperer | Coach | Healer | Speaker | Author, www.amyhackettjones.com

Grief. The one emotion we will all feel at some point in our lives. We will not escape it. But why would we? Grief is life in itself. Those we grieve live on in us and through us. Tracy's beautiful account of losing her father encapsulates the gasps of loss and the gratitude of having loved. Only one thing is eternal in this life and that is love. Tracy's beautiful book just reiterates that although in the physical we die, we will never die in the hearts of those who love us. This book is a hand on a shoulder for anyone going through bereavement during these uncertain times. Simply beautiful.

Eleana Canny, Ireland

Tracy Stone is a globally renowned clinical hypnotherapist, transformational coach and international bestselling author. Having trained and coached thousands of employees in many of the top Fortune 50 companies to radically transform their work and lives, Tracy today expands her professional horizons by using her unique talents and skills to help those suffering the loss of a loved one. She has published this deeply personal book to offer a guide through grief.

CLIENT TESTIMONIALS

Speaking to Tracy really changed my perspective and my challenges in life! I feel so much lighter now and full of energy. Thank you for literally taking a load off my shoulders.

NT, Berkshire, UK

Tracy is amazing. She helped me at a very difficult time in my life. She taught me to be happy again, believe in myself, and look forward to the future. She is someone who really cares about the person she is treating and what she does. I can't say enough good things about her!!

MB, Oxfordshire, UK

Tracy is amazing, and she is extremely good at what she does. She is a deeply caring and empathetic person, which makes her the best to truly understand and help her clients. I trust her fully and am very grateful to have found her.

RH, Buckinghamshire, UK

Tracy is so lovely — she is easy to talk to and really compassionate. She understood me instantly and helped me with exactly what I needed. The whole experience was fascinating, and it's really changed the way I think. I've made great progress and am very grateful to Tracy.

SG, Berkshire, UK

Tracy really got to the core of my issues and gave me clarity. I have been able to move on with my life with confidence and reassurance. Her advice for the future has been very beneficial. Tracy is a warm, intelligent, wise practitioner. Her techniques produce truly outstanding results.

Thank you Tracy!

PL, Dorset, UK

Tracy Stone helped me uncover my true self. I was putting negative thoughts in my head that were stopping me from reaching my potential.

Her methodology taught me how to reframe negative unconscious thoughts into positive conscious thoughts by repeating specific affirmations she customized for me. I wasn't sure how this was going to work, but after 21 days, I noticed it had a great impact in my life. I now walk confidently knowing that anything is possible if you put your mind to it. Thank you Tracy for your knowledge, patience, and guidance! I would recommend Tracy to anyone having trouble levelling up in life!

YR, Kentucky, USA

Tracy took me through a program which consisted of an initial hypnotherapy session over video call and follow-up video calls once a week to check how I was progressing. I only have positive things to say about Tracy and wish I had contacted her sooner. She made me feel at ease straight away and was very easy to talk to. I left each session feeling less anxious and more confident in myself. I would highly recommend her.

A, Berkshire, UK

Some time ago, I realized that I need to change the way I operate. I wanted to enjoy my life and lead a stress-free life. Fast-forward two months — life couldn't be any better. It now seems so simple, yet Tracy, in her calm and authentic way, had to intervene to make it happen! Recommend her to all.

B, London, UK

From the first moment I spoke with Tracy, I felt at consummate ease for the first time in many years. Having battled with addiction over a number of years, her approach to therapy is both amazing and has an immediate impact.

By working with Tracy over a very short time, I now have the self-belief and self-liking that addiction stole from me. I now identify the triggers in my life that led me on the path to addiction and how to deal with the demons.

I can never thank Tracy enough, and my only regret is that I didn't seek her support many years earlier.

Inspirational, rewarding, and a resounding benefit for everyone.

C, Berkshire, UK

Working with Tracy Stone has been absolutely transformational. She helped me to see how I had complete control of my thoughts and beliefs, which empowered me to control my life in ways I never imagined were possible. After literally decades of actions that did not support my desired outcomes, I had a breakthrough with Tracy that has changed everything. It was surprisingly simple. We all know that having the knowledge about what to do is not the same as doing it, and Tracy helped me to quickly bridge the knowing/doing gap in a loving and safe environment. A session of Rapid Transformational Therapy with Tracy, for me, felt like self-hypnosis, a deep guided meditation, years of therapy, and 1,000 hugs to my past, current, and future self... It was amazing!! I would wholeheartedly recommend Tracy Stone to anyone... Your life will never be the same.

Traci Harrell, It's All Bigger Than Me Consulting LLC,
Bellevue, Washington, USA

Tracy's RTT Therapy and coaching has helped me in a way that no testimonial can do justice to, but I will give it a go! I decided to try Rapid Transformational Therapy after deciding initially to lose weight and adopt a much healthier lifestyle, but Tracy didn't stop there! We also addressed other issues, (or roadblocks as I call them) that I had been stumbling on my whole life, such as balancing work/life issues and stress/anxiety. She made me aware of how the negative way I was talking to myself was having a detrimental effect on my overall thinking and affecting my life. From our first session, she taught me how to build a tool kit to successfully break down these blocks, get beyond them, how to succeed doing this, and more importantly, how to maintain this success. She is a delightful and warm lady that instantly puts you at ease and strikes a connection with you. She has razor-sharp perception and will pick up on the things you haven't necessarily mentioned or said in addition to the things you are discussing. Her amazing coaching skills ensure that you are kept on track in the follow-up sessions. I am extremely grateful to her and could not recommend her highly enough.

JC, Wokingham, UK

CONTENTS

INTRODUCTION

Make yourself a cup of your most comforting drink and sit with me for a while. I'm having a jasmine tea. Go on, I'll wait for you. Now, let's share a little time together.

In all likelihood you are reading this book because you have lost someone you loved dearly. So let me start by saying that I am very sorry for your loss. Truly. Whether your loss was recent or not so recent, the pain, uncertainty, and that feeling of being broken into a thousand pieces hurts like nothing else on earth. You may, at times, have found yourself struggling to make your way through this period of unfathomable and deeply unwanted change. You may have felt or still feel that the emptiness will never go away. I promise you that it's quite normal to feel this way.

Loss or grief is the provoking voice of doubt that whispers in silky conspiratorial tones, planting seeds of "I can't do this," and "Why?" or, "Now what?" and "If only..." As bespoke as a finely tailored suit, it fits everyone differently, made-to-measure so precisely that it feels like you have been sewn into it, lulling you into believing this is the only suit you will ever wear from now on. Grief is breathless. Grief constricts. It's disorienting and isolating in nature. It can shift your emotional center of gravity, swaddle you in waves of nauseating vertigo, then it pulls the rug out from underneath and slaps you in the face should you forget that... this growling, clawing, submerging, unfathomable sorrow... is... real. Too many times it's the ultimate black hole of empty numbness. It reveals itself in every conceivable and inconceivable shade between feeling everything and feeling nothing at all.

So, again, I am sorry for your loss because I know how it feels.

I have had a front row seat to grief. I have loved someone with great strength, spirit, fortitude, and passion, and lost them. I have felt bereft, lost, uncertain, and physically and emotionally maxed out as you do, *and* despite this, I have thankfully been able to slay the monster of grief. Crafting myself a cocktail of love and acceptance, in double measures, has enabled me to see clearly again. To know that life can and does go on. Love gave me the ability to be brave. Acceptance gave me fortitude.

Though you may be struggling, encountering more 'downs' than 'ups,' and questioning your ability to get through this, know that you are not alone. We will gently yet powerfully embark on this quest of healing together, to get back to feeling stronger and living with purpose again. The love you feel in your heart will soon imbibe you with the bravery and inner strength you need to begin to heal and live again. What is absolute and unfailing is that when we grieve the loss of someone so pivotal in our lives, just as you and I do, the love remains.

Give that thought a little space for a moment before you continue.

The chapters, stories, experiences, and techniques I share with you in this book are imparted with the sincere wish to help you find your way back to the resilient, loving, lovable, brave, worthy, wonderful you who your special someone loved. Back to feeling more like you again through your own very raw and very real experience with grief. If you are on that rocky road, feeling like you are walking barefoot over the jagged surface of your grief, with neither map nor compass and unequipped for the journey, or if you want to find ways to process your grief entirely on your terms and in your own words, you have come to the right place.

The sharing of deeply personal stories of others who have walked in your shoes, the insights into how and why grief has come to sit with you for a while, and the 'Baby Steps' *resilience-building actions* at the end of each chapter in this book will provide the glue to hold yourself together and gradually build your very own, personalized grief survival guide. One you can dip into on your own time, going at your pace, finding and using your own experience and words, and revisit when the notion takes you.

As we accompany each other through these pages, take comfort from the knowledge that this period of intense acclimatization is a testament to your powerful ability to love and to be loved. You have a gift, an innate capacity for love. In fact, love is one of your most incredible assets, and it will be your torch, compass, and map for the road ahead. This journey is your own personal odyssey through the grief that is unfurling. The path you have found yourself on is an organic, living, sentient thing; it changes, evolves, climbs steeply, falls away, and eventually plateaus and settles into a rhythm that *will* work for you. Adjustment to the new path ahead, confidence in yourself, and connection to those you hold dearest in your life and heart will come from a strength and resource-fulness you never even knew existed within you.

Many books, articles, and friends will, with good intentions, tell you that you won't grieve forever. They may tell you that you will feel better, stronger, and back to being you again soon. While this might sound ridiculous, trivializing, and frankly impossible when you first hear it, these well-wishers are more right than even they realize. Nevertheless, they might have underestimated that wading through it from inside of the sticky, heady heaviness of grief is hard going, unclear, and far from straightforward. It's fraught with setbacks, fears, doubts, guilt, tears, and moments when it's one step forward and two, three, or perhaps 12 steps backward.

Time *is* a great healer, but navigating grief definitely takes more than simply time.

When I first started my passage through grief, I thought I could and indeed should do this alone. That I should just put on my 'big girl pants' and cope. I thought I shouldn't *need* help. I assumed that as a clinical hypnotherapist and coach who has helped countless people from actors in Los Angeles to blue-chip CEOs in New York, Emirati heiresses, singers in Sydney, and all kinds of people everywhere in between to overcome their greatest difficulties, traumas, and blocks to happiness in life, I shouldn't need help. But it was tough. *So very tough.* There were days when there appeared to be no stopping the tears from falling or my heart from aching. My Mum, my sister Gina, and I all supported each other. My partner was the wise, steady, solid yet comforting foundation on which I knew, as always, I could depend. I was particularly fortunate and blessed to have the support I did but, despite that, I was acutely and painfully aware of a growing, festering shadow that was at times overwhelming, distressing, and shattering.

When I searched for books to read on the topic of how to overcome grief, I was bowled over by the lack of emotionally connecting yet practical, helpful books which could make sense of grief and, in turn, evoke a material difference in how people experience it.

Most books on this deeply traumatic topic tend to follow one of two primary approaches. One approach is to share a timeline of loss set out as a story, conveying you through the emotional highs and lows of a specific relationship that resulted in loss. Then, it's up to you, the reader, to find and extract your own learnings or to simply read it as a story that is perhaps reminiscent in some way of your own experience. The other approach is a more theoretical tome which will investigate, debate, hypothesize, and proffer the physical and psychological effects of grief more in the abstract than the personal. For many those approaches leave them feeling neither better nor wiser, nor with any more hope than they felt before they picked up the book in the first place.

This book is different. The magic recipe baked into the pages of *Love Remains* is as follows:

1 hefty slice of the bitter experience of loss
1 dash of supporting loved ones through their loss
2 or 3 scoops of experience helping others overcome their greatest traumas
1 cup of the generously shared experience of others
1 generous serving of clarity and understanding
1 or 2 portions of humor
1 large helping of resilience-building action steps that make a huge difference
1 large spoon of the wisdom of great minds
1 overflowing cup of love
2 heaping spoons of strength
1 cup of memories
1 healthy dose of endurance
1 liberal sprinkling of gratitude

The method for crafting and personalizing this recipe to craft your own personal guide through grief will reveal itself as you read on.

One of the things that has struck me in both my own journey and in the journeys kindly shared by others who I will introduce you to as we proceed through these pages, is the expectation we have that in order to move on with life, to cope, to no longer look or feel broken, we will have to stop mourning or grieving. Why would I do that? Why would I stop missing and mourning someone who was so important to and intricately involved in my life? I now understand that this is one of the most unreasonable, unrealistic, and unattainable objectives we can set for ourselves. In fact, it sets us up for epic failure. So don't buy into that self-sabotage of stopping yourself from feeling your unique feelings. Grief isn't a black-and-white, binary thing. It doesn't need to be something that we have to shake entirely free of to begin living our own lives again.

I have come to realize that I don't need to let go of the person I love or stop grieving and missing them in order to move forward with life and to allow happiness back in. Both these aspects of me can cohabit. Perhaps together they even make me stronger. And instead of focusing on when I will finally be free of grief, what I actually need is to find a loving and fortifying home within me for my grief to exist, and thereby, to change the nature, meaning, and effect of it. Now *that's doable*.

So, if like me you are ready to move forward, or you like the idea of finding that elusive balance in your grief, turn to the next page with me.

CHAPTER 1:

LOSING HGLD

REFLECTIONS

TRACI HARRELL

Dad, *your smile* meant everything
You helped me grow and spread my wings

Would this loss be something I could endure?
Deep in my heart I could not be sure

After time that seemed like it would not end
Waiting for the inevitable to begin

In less than one day, we were home without dad
He no longer suffered, but we were sad

Saying goodbye was hollow and touch-free
That's just how it had to be

I couldn't allow myself thinking space
We kept busy and carried ourselves with grace

We laughed and cried, all day long
The day was filled with beautiful song

Weeping for what had been a delight
Would I make it through the night?

A *Grief Guide* was needed after he left
I needed to start with *Baby Steps*

I listened to my body and held our memories tight
I knew that in time we would be alright

When I close my eyes, I can see Dad waiting in the car to collect me from the train. As usual, he must have arrived early to get his prime vantage point parking space. His face lights up as soon as he spots me in the distance, his cracked tooth smile spreading wide with the kind of glee that makes it look as if he's won the lottery. My heart lifts. I feel special. Singled out among all the other suits heading home from the office. I get a little 'pep' in my step, hold myself straighter with pride, and beam a smile back at him. I know he is chomping at the bit to get the lowdown on my day's adventures. Boy, it feels pretty damn brilliant to be this special to someone.

That's why I still can't believe HE is gone.

I mean, I know he is gone. I just can't believe it.

Every day the quietly vigilant SWAT soldier of my intense loss carefully, silently, stealthily picks his moments, swooping in to jolt me out of whatever frivolous reverie or flurry of activity I am busying myself with to remind me that *DAD IS GONE.*

These sudden attacks feel like a cruel joke played by some unseen, menacing puppeteer with a sole resolute objective to remind me, should I stray more than a few breaths from the ache that endures, that yes, my beloved Dad is gone, and he will not return. It's the knife that keeps on twisting, allowing momentary lapses in the unwanted knowledge, only to be reminded with an expert twist of that steely cold blade of truth yet again. *He is gone.*

At times it's like being swallowed by a powerful riptide, scrabbling, fighting to claw back up for air, breathing, thinking that it's all okay for a bit, it's 'doable,' then being dunked back down into the grabbing, swirling darkness again. Sometimes it's as if someone has spotted that you were inching toward 'okay' or a tiny smidgen of normality or existence and functionality, if even for a little bit, and has called you out on it saying, "Not so quick there! Don't get ahead of yourself."

So often, it feels like Dad just walked out of the room to make some cheese and Bovril™ (a super savory salty beefy extract paste he loved to indulge in) on toast or to feed the birds out on the patio and 'deadhead' the flowers and will be back in a few minutes as if nothing has happened. Oh, how I wish it were so.

You know what I mean. *You* understand. You also have been dealt a *hefty slice of the bitter experience of loss.*

We 'lost' (what a strange term that is!) Dad on the 16th of October 2020 at 12.25 PM. This man who, through my misguided notion of the immortality of those held dearest to me, I somehow expected to always be there, finally succumbed to the physical forces which had overcome and ravaged his body and mind and brutally extinguished his last droplets of will, defiance, and fight.

Dad had battled many times, rebelling, fighting, evading, and crushing the enemy forces of diabetes, heart attacks, and cancer. This time he found himself staring down the barrel, at dementia, which threatened to cut short his life. I, to this day, am quite convinced that the main inspiration, the hypnotic muse behind his motivation to survive all the health issues he endured, was his love and devotion to Mum. But, this time was different. He had no more to give. He was spent, exhausted, and ready to be set free.

Before I share more about his passing, let me rewind a little and introduce you to Dad and the gleaming Aladdin's™ cave treasures of his character. As with many daughters, I looked up to, loved, and adored him. He was special, a one-off. I may be a tad biased in my opinion, but that's okay. If you indulge my bias, I will be happy to do the same for you. Deal? He was, in the considerable majority of situations, a gentle giant. A man of great intelligence, with avid knowledge and insightful comprehension on a wealth of topics, the breadth and depth of which I will never fully appreciate. He was quietly cultured, something which he hid from many who enjoyed his company, preferring to entertain those around him with his boyish humor and his ability to tell the same joke or story over and over... and over again.

He had a twinkle in his eye for fun and mischief which was simply unrivaled and throughout his lifetime remained unquenchable. This thirst for devilment and wisecracks sparked him into relaying tall tales when he had even the smallest of audiences. A prime example was when Gina, my older sister, and I were young, doe-eyed, and gullible, he boldly informed us that our uncles included the likes of Bing Crosby and Bob Hope and would regale us with the intricate, entertaining, and entirely fictitious adventures they all had together. He was so convincing, empathetic, and sincere in his storytelling that we fell for it hook, line and sinker. We so effectively bought into the fabulous fabrication that we would relay it to all our friends for years to come, encouraged by his continued elaborate ability to stay in character. Somehow, it never occurred to us in our innocence that for Bing and Bob to be our uncles, they would have had to be his brothers. Not to mention that they were both born in 1903, 37 years before Dad made his appearance. Let's just say he was very convincing and ready at a moment's notice to spin some colorful yarn.

He loved music and would become enraptured by the classics, having technical familiarity with and love for particular pieces to the degree that he would know not only the composer, the name of the piece, or what the specific section of the piece of music was called, but also who the conductor, orchestra, or soloist was and would hold spirited debates about who brought the magic out of the composition. While driving, he would embrace his inner method acting composer, using one hand to majestically and passionately control his unseen orchestra. This was generally the same multitasking exuberant hand he would also use to extend huge and jovially audacious waves out the window at anyone he passed. He equally loved more modern classics with a diverse auditory palate ranging from the angel-voiced Katherine Jenkins. the sophisticated Shirley Bassey, Sarah Brightman's pure operatic tones, Matt Monro's swinging tap-along tunes, Louis Armstrong's trumpet-fueled and gravelly throated jazz, the powerfully emotional mastery of Andrea Bocelli, all the way to anything played and conducted by Andre Rieu.

Dad loved to read and was never to be found without a book. Sometimes they were dynamic and intellectual business biopics but more often than not they were the fictitious, heroic escapades of the likes of Ian Fleming's prolific British Secret Service agent James Bond or Tom Clancy's CIA analyst turned field operative, Jack Ryan.

His mind was so rich, so full of 'smarts,' so alive and ever-expanding that it was like a sponge that was never quenched. Having a mind like his was like having a greyhound that needed constant exercise. He fed that need by building a brilliant career in a number of food processing industries where he started out in his early 20s as a bright-eyed and bushy-tailed junior on the management track of Dennys™ (Henry Denny & Sons), one of Ireland's most prolific meat processing businesses. Dad believed in being very hands-on, becoming an expert in all facets of the huge factories which were his playground of adventure, education, and inspiration. He led teams of hundreds and, never one to stay in the 'ivory tower' of his office, he would patrol every area regularly, knowing how important it was to be 'in' the business, not just on top of it. He turned his hand from designing complex production machinery to creating finely balanced meat curing recipes, to negotiating with the Japanese on their turf after a long night of sake and sushi, and then just as easily would roll up his sleeves to fillet a fish on the production line, much to the amusement of the production line operatives, particularly as he was infinitely faster and more precise than they were! He never expected anyone to do anything he wasn't able or willing to do, but he drove his people hard to get the best for and from them. I can hear him now, just as he did then, demanding quality and pride in the work of his people, saying, "If you're going to do something... do it right!"

He went on to set up his own factory where he bravely and astutely began to process not only the abundant fresh fish found around the exquisite Irish coast but also their by-products, which up until then had been viewed as waste by all other similar businesses. These by-products included the fish roe, which he exported to other countries who viewed the roe as a delicacy. After selling his business, Dad's final career move was as a much sought-after consultant specializing in meat and fish processing, rising to the top and solving complex problems as effortlessly and mesmerizingly as a master conductor elevating his orchestra to stratospheric levels.

Dad was also a diabetic who never met an ice cream he didn't love and who found it pretty much impossible to turn a blind eye to heaping hunks of pavlova, his favorite dessert consisting of clouds of sugary meringue mounded high with whipped cream and sprinkled with juicy fresh berries and little rivulets of sweet fruit-flavored coulis. Huge steaks, charred far beyond what any chef would allow out of their kitchen, were a thing of pure unadulterated pleasure for him. When he was enjoying his food, which he *really* did, the sheer pleasure he experienced would invariably result in his eyes blissfully rolling up in his head. No words were necessary. His expression told us he was in his happy place.

He was an adoring husband to my mother. He was so totally besotted with her that he would constantly inform us in our childhood any time we were at odds with Mum (just doing our job as growing little ones!): "Whether your mother is right or wrong, she is always right." Blind faith. Willingly given. Absolute trust. It's a rare thing.

Mum and Dad did everything together. They had been married for 54 amazing years. He, up until his final few years, had been a true-blue alpha of a man. The driver. The breadwinner. Butch Cassidy to her Sundance Kid. Batman to her Robin. The formidable rock on which Mum relied on. He had always made her feel safe.

He was a loving Dad to my sister and me. What he lacked in time spent with us during the working week, he made up for in his ability to shift instantly into fantastical creative mode, so a Sunday drive would become a 'magical mystery tour.' On journeys to anywhere beyond our local environs, we would ask, as all children do, "How much further?" and the answer was inevitably and always 74 and ¼ miles. It didn't matter if it was two or 200 miles in reality. During those drives, he would sing along to the old eight-track tape in the car and tell endless made-up-on-the-spot fairy tales.

To me, he was HGLD. I had called him HGLD since my mid-20's, which is half my lifetime ago. It was just something that came to me when I was writing a poem about him when he had suffered a heart attack and was scheduled for triple bypass (coronary artery bypass graft) surgery. My *Handsome God-Like Dad*. It stuck. He seemed to revel in it, even naming his consultancy business HGLD Limited. It was our little inside joke, and I would swear that it gave him a youthful pep in his step.

The innocence and awe that often comes with being the daughter of such a force of nature meant that I somehow never expected anything about him to change. I never expected for him to ever be less than the powerful, inspiring, and sharp-witted hero he had always been to me. It wasn't until he reached his mid-70s that Dad started to become aware that his cognition was playing tricks on him. I would with good intentions tell him not to worry about forgetting a name, place, or event. I told him that we all do that, and it's human nature. Looking back, it's with some anguish that I realize how frustrating that must have been for him to keep hearing, all the time knowing deep inside his heart and mind that something was wrong.

After a year or two of steadily increasing forgetfulness and deep frustration at his inability to find words and to put names to simple, mundane things, Dad, at the age of 76, was diagnosed with vascular dementia. On average, people with vascular dementia live for around five years after symptoms begin. Mum wisely chose to withhold the diagnosis from him, knowing that if it was confirmed it would stress him more, and his powers of reasoning and logic were already dramatically impacted. Still, he sensed what was coming for him, and it frightened him. What a thought — HGLD frightened of anything! It seems such a cruel twist of fate for someone whose mind had been an effervescent motor, razor-sharp and insatiable, to be cut down mercilessly by his ultimate foe and to lose his greatest power; his mind.

Being a practical man, a man who thought and planned forward and a myopically adoring and protective husband, Dad knew that, quite literally, life-altering change was on the horizon for both him and Mum. So, he planned as best as he knew how to ensure Mum would be sur-rounded by family when the time would come for him to "shuffle off this mortal coil," as he would often put it, quoting Hamlet. They moved from the home they loved in the countryside, surrounded by birds they enjoyed feeding and watching daily, from the area of Wexford in the 'sunny' southeast of Ireland where Dad was born and grew from boy to man, up to the lush, green midlands of Ireland so Mum would be settled in a more manageable house, in the town for amenities, and most importantly, near her sister, many cousins, and her always willing-to-help nephews and their families.

The move took a huge toll on Dad's health. He also endured debilitating pain from previously unhealed issues resulting from his colon cancer of several years before. In the weeks leading up to their move to the midlands, he was in so much discomfort and intense pain that he had to spend most of each day and night lying at a particular angle. This resulted in pressure sores which, nine months later, in the height of COVID-19, became infected and Dad ended up in hospital. *This, for our family, was the beginning of the end.*

By this time, Dad was totally dependent on Mum in every way. Soon, the roles he and Mum played in each other's lives swapped with Mum stepping up to take care of many of the things Dad used to, such as being the designated driver and watchful caretaker. To his constant frustration and confusion, he had reached the stage of not comprehend-ing what things were or what to do with them. He had taken to putting the electric kettle in the sink to wash it and boiling bananas thinking they were something entirely different. Mum had to keep a watchful eye on his every move in an effort to allow him to still do things while keeping him safe. When she left the room for even a few minutes, on her return, Dad would say how he had missed her and thought she was never coming back. His ability to find words, understand what things were and what to do with them to measure time all had been stolen from him in his slippery decline into dementia.

Due to the ongoing ravaging of the COVID-19 pandemic, no visitors were allowed into the hospital. As unfortunate as that is for any patient, it was devastating, confusing, and alienating for those suffering, like Dad, from dementia. He was stuck in a ward with people he didn't know, not understanding why he was there, and certainly not understanding why he wasn't with Mum.

He reached a point where he demanded to be released home but, once he got his wish, he remained there for a mere two days before being returned by ambulance to the hospital. Mum embarked on a daily mission to drop off home-cooked food, clean pajamas, and a handwritten love letter for him, leaving his care package with a porter or nurse and praying for news and updates on his condition.

Gina and I desperately wanted and needed to be with Mum and Dad to look after them, but with both of us living in the United Kingdom and with considerable travel restrictions within and between both countries, it was far from straightforward to plan the trip. We waited impatiently, checking daily for news if travel through Wales was being allowed so we could each drive our own cars across England, through Wales, and onto the ferry which would take us to Ireland and our parents. Eventually, we made the trip on the 13th of July, 2020.

At this stage, we all expected that Dad would soon be moved from the hospital to a respite care center for a couple of weeks before coming home to where he desperately wanted to be. This was sadly not in the cards.

As soon as we reached our parent's home in Portlaoise, County Laois, some 95 kilometers southwest of Dublin, and started learning more about the gravity of Dad's situation, it quickly became clear that Plan A, Dad's return home, was as practical as a scrunched-up piece of paper tossed into the waste bin. We quickly moved on to evolve Plan B, which entailed getting Dad out of the hospital where he had become so alienated from everyone and everything he loved and understood and moving him to a nursing home for better care. His feelings of abandonment in the hospital had led him to do something he had never even come close to doing before — *he had given up all hope*. Detrimentally, he had also given up eating. We wanted him brought home where we knew he would be happier but were instructed with absolute clarity by all the nurses and doctors we pleaded with that his medical care would be prohibitive and, in reality, impossible from home. It simply wouldn't have resulted in the best care for him. We were painfully conflicted. We wanted Dad to be home in Portlaoise with Mum, where we knew he wanted to be. But, we also wanted the best care for him. The care that would give him his only chance of survival. This stark set of options forced our hand, and we went for Dad's only shot at survival; move him from the hospital to a nursing home.

My sister and I both felt painfully limited in what we could do to help as we were making our way slowly through the mandatory 14-day home quarantine after entering the country, enforced as a means to control the spread of the worldwide pandemic.

By sheer coincidence, or perhaps it was God or The Universe finally cutting us a break, the first day after our quarantine ended, Wednesday the 29th of July 2020, was the day Dad was taken by ambulance from the hospital in Portlaoise to a wonderful nursing home in Athy, County Kildare, a neighboring county. None of us, at the time, realized it would be his final home.

The caring staff at the impeccably maintained nursing home busied themselves welcoming and settling Dad into the loveliest corner room with lots of windows allowing him to see all the comings and goings.

Every single one of the nurses and the considerable army of support staff were simply wonderful. Nothing was ever too much trouble for them. If Dad refused his food, they would take it away and offer him anything that could be made in their kitchen, anything at all. The most he could manage would be a few spoonfuls of ice cream, but his ability and willingness to eat even a chocolate-coated Magnum™ ice cream, his slam dunk favorite, dwindled quickly. Mum, through special permission of the matron (the dedicated, experienced, and compassionate woman in charge of the entire nursing home), was allowed to visit Dad daily at lunchtime to encourage him to eat something, anything, just a tiny mouthful. We knew it was an uphill struggle to convince him that eating was even remotely sensible but, still, it meant time for him with the love of his life.

A week after Dad's arrival at the nursing home, we had settled into the daily journeys from Portlaoise to Athy and back home again. That Friday, Mum, Gina, and I were back in Mum's house in Portlaoise after our daily visit to see Dad. Our dinner was nearly ready, and Mum had switched on the TV to catch the 6 PM news. In the time it took the presenter to solemnly update us with the breaking news headlines, our already stressful situation had just been further complicated with the announcement that a government-issued COVID-19 lockdown was to be enforced that same night at midnight. This devastating news threatened to prevent us from getting access to Dad, whose nursing home was in an adjacent county. Mum just slumped into the sofa, looking tiny and frail with torrents of tears rolling down her cheeks. Broken. Seeing Mum's lifeline to Dad come crashing down in a landslide jolted me like an electric shock out of my own dazed moment. I pushed away the fearful voice in my head warning me that I might not get to see my adored Dad again. I would have to focus on what this meant to me later; just then, the first priority for both Gina and me was Mum and how to get her to Dad.

My sister and I sprang into action. Gina immediately reached out to the nursing home to negotiate Mum's continued permission to visit Dad despite the new restrictions. I was calling hotels, guesthouses,

B&Bs; anything with a bedroom for rent in the area. My sister worked her magic with the matron, promising anything for Mum to be allowed to have contact with Dad. I managed to find one guesthouse willing to help us. All other accommodations were locking their doors that night.

We didn't know when we would get to see Mum next or, once the lockdown came into force at midnight that very night, if we would be able to make the 30-minute journey from County Laois, where Mum lived, to County Kildare, where Dad's nursing home was. Gina had quickly made a substantial care package for Mum of everything she might conceivably need to help her feel safe and prepared for an unknown amount of time away from her own home. Together, the three of us loaded her car up and bundled Mum into the driving seat to set off in the dark to her new 'digs' for the foreseeable future. After programming my satellite navigation for our new destination, I led the way in my car with a thousand thoughts fighting for space in my head. Gina, who would be invaluable as a calming and confident navigator, accompanied Mum, who was shaken and being carried along by the momentum of the surreal, almost dystopian situation.

Despite feeling sick to her stomach with uncertainty, discomfort, and fear, Mum was resolute in wanting to be wherever she needed to be so she could get to Dad. That was our priority, and we were thoroughly grateful to have a feasible plan. Mum bravely lied and told us she would be fine, but her worried face told us the truth. She was scared, exhausted, and knew that things would get worse before they would get better. Gina and I dashed back to my car and put the pedal to the floor to ensure we crossed back into County Laois just minutes before the midnight deadline brought the new restrictions into force.

So began a completely new routine for us all, making it up as we went along, slashing through every setback that dared separate us from Dad. At first, Mum was the only one of us allowed into the nursing home for around an hour per day at lunchtime. She would don her PPE (Personal Protective Equipment) and spend treasured time with Dad daily, at first just that hour, but then eventually the staff allowed her visits to last as long as she wanted. She would chat with Dad, read her magazines or newspaper, watch TV, and sometimes have a snooze in the chair beside him. They held hands, and Mum constantly soothed his worries as best she could. This was what he needed — his security blanket.

Still, he resisted eating. We could all see him disappearing from us; physically, mentally, and emotionally. His recognition of my sister and I would come and go, and he became adept at pretending he knew who we were. There would be flickers of awareness, little tantalizing moments of 'Dadness' giving us hope only to be dashed moments later with vacancy and confusion. It gives us great comfort to believe, as we do, that he continued to recognize Mum and mostly to understand who she was, though, at times in his altered jigsaw of a mind, he mistook her for his own mother. That was more than okay by us all. Dad's mother had died far too young when he was only 3 years old. He had no memories of her, but he treasured one precious photograph. It was a family photo onto which his father had arranged for a photographer to graft a picture of his mother. He loved that picture, and I think as the end grew near, it had become less of a two-dimensional photo and more of a real, tangible, living family setting for him.

Knowing that the lockdown rules prohibited travel outside of the area we were staying in, we asked the Gardai (Irish police) if we would be allowed to make the journey to the nursing home on compassionate grounds. Seeing our desperation and sincerity, they endearingly told us to go for it! They explained that the success of our journey across county lines would be up to the discretion of any individual Garda at checkpoints along the way. Hearteningly, they also said they would be very surprised if we were not allowed to pass through once we explained our situation. Their answer became our 'access all areas passport;' we grabbed it with both hands and set out the next day. Our hearts were beating fast and we were eagle-eyed as we approached the border. No Gardai were there and nobody stopped us. We felt like we were on a clandestine mission of national importance. We hadn't told Mum in case our mission failed so she was flabbergasted to see us drive into the nursing home car park. We already knew that we wouldn't be allowed inside the nursing home because of the restrictions necessitated by COVID-19 to safeguard the staff and residents. That didn't deter us, not even a smidge.

As Gina and I hurried from my car toward the outside windows of Dad's corner room, my heart lifted, and I knew with utmost certainty that we had done the right thing in coming when I saw the relief and solidarity in Mum's eyes. So began our new regular routine, a routine that gave us the contact we desperately needed and the feeling that Gina and I were doing something helpful. Despite the window that separated us, I like to think that because of our daily visit to the nursing home, Mum felt a little stronger and less alone.

The daily excursion Gina and I took across some of the most soul-expanding, breathtakingly exquisite countryside to be found anywhere on earth was nature's living, breathing calendar, signifying the rapid passage of time. The landscape we were blessed to traverse was forged from a master's palette of a million and one shades of green and, being lovingly tended by its dedicated caretakers, no two days revealed the same view. Fields transitioned from standing proud with crops of glorious Irish produce reaching upward to the sky one day to being harvested by enormous shiny machinery the next, then to rich soil, the earth's finest caviar, and back to the fresh pale green growth of youth and promise in what felt like the click of a finger. Every day's rearranged view reminded me that life was precious and ever-changing. Despite my desire to pause and bask in the beauty around me, another day had passed. I was uplifted by the journey but equally conscious that I was also fighting the clock. I didn't know how many more journeys I would have, each one ripping a page from the calendar of Dad's life.

Gina and I settled into a regular routine, meeting Mum in the car park of the nursing home and sitting with her for a short while to enjoy a takeaway coffee and a catch-up before she would go sit with her Bobby. This was much-needed time for Mum to be around her own family and a small respite in the days filled with fear, despair, exhaustion, love, and adoration. Then, when we could see Mum had arrived into Dad's room, resplendent in swamping medical blue PPE overalls, we would appear at his windows to monitor his progress, chat, sing, tell stories, and act silly; anything we could do to cheer them both up and to give Dad something to cling onto as he slipped further away from us. Come rain or shine, Gina and I would be there day in, day out, knowing that our hopes and dreams of him ever returning home had been diminished, smashed to smithereens, and were mere dust motes in the air.

Before long, the nursing staff saw that Mum needed a break; she was clearly exhausted existing in this all-consuming bubble. She needed rest — a change of environment from that one room with all its uniquely medical smells and looming reality. They agreed to allow Gina and me to take turns in Mum's place so she could have a day off twice each week.

We were thrilled to have been given this gift of time with Dad. We could sit all day and talk to him, read to him, sing, joke, take quiet time, just be there with him. That time was worth more to me than all the money, gold, or diamonds in the world. For brief but diminishing moments, I saw a tiny spark of my HGLD. He would tap his hand in time to the music I played him. He would roll his eyes in silent jest at the constant nonsensical calls of other residents, most of who were also suffering from dementia in the nearby rooms and the old lady who kept mistaking his room for hers. This fleeting proof that he was still Dad gave me something to cling onto. I treasured those moments when we could communicate an entire unspoken conversation with a conspiratorial look and raising our eyebrows at each other. There was nothing I wouldn't have done to offer him just a pinch of comfort or happiness.

All the while, Dad was rapidly declining. Fading before my eyes. Slipping away like a wisp of air that's impossible to hold onto. He had not eaten for many weeks, even refusing the protein and vitamin-infused drinks which both the staff and we tried so hard to persuade him to sip. I had succumbed to the knowledge that any slim chance of his recovery or even survival depended on him finding some way to take in protein. He was long past any chance to insert a feeding tube, and we knew it wasn't what he wanted.

I felt so powerless. I was frustrated, angry, defiant, and humbled at how inconsequential it made me feel. How can I be so strong, so successful in my career, achieving incredible things, and yet so impotent in my ability to help my own father? I could move mountains but not make things better for Dad. My silent screams were hidden under layers of smiles, jokes, positivity, and routine.

The unsolicited knowledge which kept raising its voice in the deafening silence of absolute truth (as much as I kept batting it away) resurfaced, demanding my attention. Dad was *not* coming home. He was *not* getting better. He was running out of borrowed time, and there were only a precious few grains of sand left slipping through the timer of his life.

In those last few days, the days when we had finally realized, accepted, and thought we had come to terms with letting Dad slip away, Mum, Gina, and I gathered around him. We were then joined in our vigil by my partner Simon, my niece Ciara, and my brother-in-law Ian who each traveled over from the United Kingdom. Outside Dad's window were more loving family members, painfully and lovingly looking on, wanting Dad to know they were there for him. We each were willing a miracle to happen. Wishing his agony would end. Wanting peace, comfort, and release for him. Letting him slip away? As if I had any control over the situation. My internal, unvoiced yet deafening frustration at my powerlessness, my inability to find a way to help Dad get better, or to at least wash away his pain and distress was voracious and dizzying. How could this be happening?

I waited. Watching. Unsure. A jagged lump of anguish in my throat made it impossible to breathe. It was as if I was subconsciously following Dad's labored breathing. None of us knew if it would be his last. After an eerie silence, we all looked at each other wondering if he had gone, only to hear him take another agonizing, wretched, rasping, wild-eyed, sickeningly gurgling breath in vain. It was barbarous. It was cruel. It was heartbreaking.

It wasn't like you see in the movies; a shared loving look of readiness, a last breath, and then peace. No. It was a cruel, tortured, panicked, fearful, wild-eyed, and confused scrabble for breath as his lungs flooded and his eyes locked onto Mum's. She held him, reassuring him, adoring him, unspoken words flashing between them. We all sought to comfort Dad, to tell him it was okay to go, that his own mother, father, brother, and so many other long-passed loved ones were waiting to welcome him into their arms.

Then, finally, silence.

He was gone.

It was 12.25 PM on Friday, the 16th of October, 2020. He was free. Free of pain. Free of fighting for breath. Free of fear. He was now in the arms of his long-departed mother. Safe. Whole again. We, on the other hand, had lost an irreplaceable treasure. In a nanosecond, my world had irrevocably shifted. Nothing would be the same again.

The nursing home staff came to do what they needed to do, quietly, carefully, sadly, kindly. The reality hadn't hit home for any of us.

Then, with tears rolling silently but ceaselessly down my cheeks and my head reeling dizzily from the confusion it struggled to make sense of — that Dad was actually gone — abruptly, it was time for action. What a bizarre thing to have to suddenly 'do stuff' and go through a list of things that had to be done right there, right then. We started making calls and sending messages to inform the people who loved Dad so dearly and were watching, waiting, and praying.

Gina and I called the undertaker (not a thing I ever imagined having to do). I was amazed how, even in the darkest of moments, taking action gets one through those moments. I focused on getting through one moment, then another, then another. *Baby steps.*

I drove to my parent's house for the first time in several days, as we had been staying day and night by Dad's side, to collect the clothes and other bits and pieces the undertaker would need. On my way back to the nursing home, I indulged in some uplifting recollections of Dad: so proudly matching up his shirts and ties and always having a freshly ironed, crisp white handkerchief in his pocket — ever the dapper gentleman.

In what felt to me like the blink of an eye, the quietly respectful undertaker gently wheeled Dad out of the nursing home. The short path from Dad's room right beside the exit door to the discreetly dark vehicle that solemnly waited for him was lined with almost every member of the staff, all wanting to say farewell to one of their wards, someone they had lovingly cared for and cared about. I didn't want this moment to end, for us to have to leave these amazing people because somehow that would make it more real and finite.

Then, in another blink of an eye, we were in our cars and on our way home... without Dad. Each of us was exhausted, yet we all had long lists of things requiring our immediate attention: arrangements to be made, decisions to be taken, and messages to be sent and responded to. I drove silently, but on the inside I was screaming, asking myself how this could have happened.

The COVID-19 pandemic was like a tidal wave and swept away the rituals many of us were relying on as key steps, customs, anchors, and rites of passage through grief. Gatherings with loved ones sharing their condolences and love were no longer allowed. No wake. No procession. No church filled with family and friends. No hugs. Not even a handshake was allowed. I knew exactly what Dad, a practical man in many ways, would counsel me, "Well, luvvie, you have to deal with reality, with what it is, not what you wish it was, and just do your best."

In Ireland, still a predominantly Catholic country, most funerals happen on the third day after the death. Mum was bereft and exhausted from months of stress, worry, fear, and endless days and evenings spent watching the only man she had ever loved fade away to be replaced by a confused, frustrated, unfamiliar shell of the Titan HGLD was.

We had less than three days to plan a funeral that would do justice to Dad, with no previous experience to guide us. Dad had left a list of his favorite tunes that he wanted to be played at his 'send off'... but who knew there were so many versions of "Ave Maria"? It was important that we got this right for him. Simple complexities consumed our time, such as figuring out how to incorporate the songs he had wanted but which weren't hymns and therefore couldn't be played in the church. We pored and deliberated over the many options for readings and prayers for the service. The funeral day was racing toward us with the terrifying, threatening, thundering power of a train bearing down and ramping up speed with lights blazing and whistles screaming like a banshee through a dark tunnel. This focus of energy and attention was a convenient way for me to avoid accepting what was at the crux of it all; *HE was gone*. My precious HGLD wasn't coming back.

Not being allowed to have a big traditional Irish wake for Dad during COVID-19 was both a blessing and a missed opportunity. A blessing in that we didn't have to make small talk. We didn't have to entertain and console a ceaseless stream of kind visitors who would have come to pay their condolences and respects and to share their animated memories of escapades with Dad. We didn't have to make endless pots of tea, pour pegs of whiskey, make sandwiches, or smile. We didn't have to face other people and their very well-intentioned sympathy or grief. Instead, we remained as insular as possible, avoiding face-to-face conversations that were sure to bring tears that we didn't know how to contain. We focused on the many text messages we had to send to let people know Dad had passed. We made and answered countless phone calls with the people who had known and loved Dad. We just wanted to get through these three fleeting days before we had to let him go.

The missed opportunity was that being surrounded by others would have allowed us to get out of our own heads. Listening to them and allowing them to share their feelings and colorful recollections of Dad would have kept us mentally, emotionally, and physically occupied. I thought of the saying, "Idle hands are the Devil's playground," and knew that I needed to keep not only my hands busy but my mind. I couldn't afford to leave myself too much thinking space when I wasn't ready to process my immense loss. Not yet anyway.

In lieu of a proper wake, the musically blessed Smyth branch of our family, known as the 65 Kitchen Choir, arranged a socially distanced concert in the pretty shrub-bordered back garden of my parent's home in Portlaoise, which was attended by a limited few of our nearest and dearest friends and family. They set up, as if in a concert hall complete with instruments, amplifiers, and microphones, right outside Dad's bedroom window and poured their hearts into every note they played and sang. Dad laid there surreally and peacefully reposing the day before his funeral. Unwilling to leave his side, Mum, Gina, Ciara, and I remained in his bedroom, clinging to each other, as the large windows flung open to the foreboding wintry elements, allowing the beautiful music in. Our tears flowed freely, but our breath fought against the growing lumps in our throats.

The music flowed... ethereal, magical, heartfelt, sad, happy, joyous, beautiful songs. At one point, it even became like a comedy sketch, giving us a desperately needed reprieve from the emotional depths, as Mum's cousin Ann, a dear member of both the Smyth family and band, began ad-libbing one of the songs Dad used to sing to Mum's younger sisters when they were little girls. It was beautifully, bizarrely poignant, and magically timely that we could all laugh together at the silliness and sincerity of it. Dad would have loved every moment and lapped it up, singing along and encouraging Ann with his own cheeky ad-libs. I could feel both his reassuring presence and his painful absence in equal measures as my tears warmed my cheeks in the cold room.

In retrospect, I recognize that all the planning, organizing, emails, phone calls, texts, revisions, practicing — the busyness — was a good thing. Necessary even. It got me through those days. It galvanized me for making the emotionally testing 121-kilometer trip from my parent's home in Portlaoise in the beautiful Irish midlands to Wexford on the 'sunny southeast' coast and the church Dad had frequented as a boy. I drove, with Mum and her cousin Ann as my passengers, directly behind the sleek and shiny hearse carrying him away from us, closely followed by Gina, her husband Ian, and Ciara, then a short cortege of family cars. It was a trip which, at Dad's own request, would take a deeply meaningful detour via the Beechdale Garden Centre in Clonroche, most particularly it's wonderful Wildflower Cafe, which Mum and Dad would visit daily before they relocated to the midlands a year before Dad passed. This was their home from home, their social hub, and where they felt surrounded by friends and fun. On that morning, we slowly and sorrowfully followed Dad on his final journey 'home.' It was a route that would also take a small final detour and respectful pause outside the home where he was born and raised.

Homeward bound in every sense.

As we approached the turn from the main road onto the smaller country road where the entrance to the garden center welcomes all, my breath was instantly crushed out of me by the sight of an endless stream of friends, neighbors, and staff from the cafe and the garden center itself lining both sides of the usually busy main road and a police roadblock ahead to quietly allow these friends to say a final farewell to one of their own. The loyal gathering accompanied us on each side of the road and walked alongside our cortege from the main road to the entrance. Their eyes told us more than their words ever could have. Their presence, socially distanced due to COVID-19 but definitely there, opened the floodgates to both our appreciation and sorrow in a way that our previous three days of activity had skilfully avoided.

I took the left turn at walking speed and eventually rolled to a gentle stop some 100 yards later at the entrance to the place Dad so loved, right behind him, with no discernible oxygen in my lungs and clear vision entirely obscured and obliterated by the burning tears that just fell like a silent waterfall. Dad's friends took turns approaching the window separating them from his peaceful, pain-free body and placing a gentle hand on the glass, saying a quiet prayer, or blowing a kiss. Their outpouring of love only served to reinforce our immense loss but in a way that supported us all and told us that he would never be forgotten. I was overwhelmingly touched to know that Dad, whether in body or spirit, will always be one of theirs.

The closer we got to the church, the heavier the rain poured. As my windscreen wipers picked up speed, I recall having a fleeting notion that the weather, by divine intervention, was echoing my emotions. By the time I had parked and was numbly making my way past family and friends who couldn't join Dad or us inside the church, the rain was a torrent of wet bullets. Fitting.

Only 25 people were allowed inside to attend the funeral service that left many standing outside. These friends, family, and acquaintances patiently, uncomplainingly, and loyally huddled under large black umbrellas near the church door.

Inside the church, we each did our very best for Dad. We wanted to, as we would say back home, 'do him proud.' I stood there in front of the gathering, barely able to believe that Dad was lying cold and lifeless in the polished coffin to my left. The very notion of it was so eye-widening, jarring, and completely inconceivable to me. Pushing down my tears, I searched for breath, and with all the control I could muster from deep inside, recited a reading. I looked from person to person, their loss and sadness clear in their solemn faces, and I took comfort from seeing how loved Dad was. Ciara, so strong and compassionate, eloquently delivered a reading and prayers of the faithful with poise and feeling beyond anything the small congregation imagined was possible. The most heartwarming part of the service was the soulful sound Gina cre-ated by singing a haunting rendition of "Ag Criost An Siol," an exquisite hymn, half in English and half in Gaeilge, the lilting Irish language. I know it took a lot out of her to stand in front of an audience, let alone at her father's funeral. I knew at that moment that Dad was there with us, nodding his head in time with the magical notes, his eyes closed and focused on the beautiful sound. He was proud of us.

Before long I found myself outside the church in the stinging rain and then, all too quickly, I was driving once more like being carried on a wave, following Dad in the hearse on our way to Dublin for our final farewell and to meet his wishes to be cremated. My eyes remained fixed on him through my windshield. I was driving as if I was sensing rather than seeing the road, with its turns, signals, traffic, and noise. All that mattered just then was that I still had him nearby.

Having had a short but evocative service allowed Gina and I to reminisce with the small group inside the crematorium on some of our favorite memories of Dad. We played a carefully curated selection of his most loved songs, until suddenly and naively unexpectedly with a bewildering and shocking finality to each of us, the curtains closed. Forever separating us from someone we dearly wanted to cling to. It was so abrupt. Frightening. Too soon. Mum dissolved in tears, and the agony was contagious. I could hear Dad's constant instruction to us since we were children ringing in my ears, telling me, "Look after your mother." Gina, Ciara, and I surrounded Mum, and we held onto each other tightly with Gina and I sharing a look that said we both knew this was just the beginning of our grief.

When it comes to the inescapable final moments of a blazing, twinkling star, it's so very hard to say goodbye knowing you will never see someone so pivotal in your life ever again. I have come to realize that it's simply not optional. That realization offers up a dual-sided gift; acceptance because it's not optional, and pain because it's unwanted.

Keeping to the day's schedule had somehow helped me up until that point to hold the reality and permanence of what was happening in a tenuously covered box in my mind. It was as if going through all these motions and rites, focusing on the organization, the activities, driving, prayers, hymns, and songs was somehow delaying what I only later realized was inevitable. I wasn't ready to let him go.

However, it wasn't my choice or within my control. For me, realizing that I was not in control turned out to be a vital piece of the puzzle to begin to deal with this great loss. Losing a loved one is never a 'choice.' But there comes a point when there's nothing more that can be done to prevent it.

I was shattered, exhausted, and fearful for how our family would acclimatize to a world without Dad, and I was running on emotional fumes as I drove the final leg of the day's journey from Dublin back to where we started early that morning in Portlaoise. As we arrived back to the house, each of us were tense, weary, uncertain, bewildered, relieved, devastated, bereft; all experiencing our own cocktail of emotions and reactions.

What I thought was the end of something big, after those harrowing months, was in fact only the beginning of something even bigger. The beginning of a decidedly customized, wildly fluctuating, Bermuda Trianglesque journey through grief. It was real. It was the end. I had no more tasks scheduled to separate me from this inevitable farewell which I would have walked over hot coals to delay for even just one more moment. There was no longer a list to keep me occupied. I had to shift from all the 'doing' into allowing the reality to settle into place; what was once a living, breathing, tactile connection to my dearly loved HGLD had been spirited away from me to be replaced, at least for now, with sadness, separation, and an unfillable space in my heart.

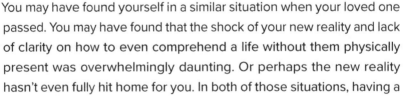

You may have found yourself in a similar situation when your loved one passed. You may have found that the shock of your new reality and lack of clarity on how to even comprehend a life without them physically present was overwhelmingly daunting. Or perhaps the new reality hasn't even fully hit home for you. In both of those situations, having a list of time-sensitive tasks to complete may prove to be exactly what you need to get through that first difficult stage of your loss.

Sometimes you just need to *focus on the things that need to be done* because that's exactly what carries you through from one minute to the next, one foot in front of the other.

"When you are sorrowful look again in your heart, and you shall see that in truth you are weeping for that which has been your delight."

KAHLIL GIBRAN

BABY STEPS

The objective of *Love Remains* and the experiences and learnings shared with you throughout these pages is to make a real, tangible, positive, empowering, and comforting difference in your life.

While you can glean much from simply reading, connecting with the journeys others have taken through their loss and finding some hope and inspiration for your own journey will help you truly maximise the healing resilience available to you by taking action.

In the same way as reading a recipe book can offer you great ideas, there is really no substitute for actually baking the cake. The transformational experience is to be found in *taking action.*

This is why I have created the *Baby Steps* resilience-building exercises which you will find at the end of each chapter. These Baby Steps are specially designed to help you to take small, 'doable' actions that move you ever closer, day-by-day, toward regaining your confidence and balance and to gradually building your very own personalized grief survival guide.

Each exercise is designed to help you to personalize the book, to tailor it to your thoughts, words, and feelings, and to gently, baby step by baby step, bring you back to you again.

Here's your first *Baby Step....*

MANAGING MY SPOONS:

As with many people dealing with grief, you may have found you have less energy and stamina than before your loved one passed. This will not always be the case but, at least for now, it's one of the ways your body is protecting you and allowing you the time and space to heal and get stronger again.

So, if you aren't already, it's time to start listening to your body and give it what it needs. Healthy food, fresh air, moderate exercise, and quality rest.

This is where the "Spoon Theory" comes into play. It's the brainchild of Christine Miserandino, an award-winning writer, blogger, and speaker, who lives with lupus, a chronic autoimmune disease.

In her theory, which was simply thought up in reply to her friend's question about the realities of living with a chronic illness, Christine described the limited energy she has by using spoons as a unit of energy. Why spoons? Well, she happened to be in a café at the time and, searching for something physical to help her explain how she felt, she gathered the nearby spoons and used them to represent finite units of energy.

Christine explained how her energy was affected by many things such as stress levels, sleeping habits, nutrition, and pain. She then handed all the 'energy' spoons she had gathered up to her friend and subsequently asked her friend to take her through a normal day for *her*. As her friend recounted all her tasks in her normal day, Christine took spoons or 'energy' away for each task, varying by the amount of energy the task would consume from her. Some tasks consumed one spoon, others more. Long before her friend had finished listing her daily tasks, she had run out of spoons. Her friend then realized how for Christine living with chronic pain meant she had fewer spoons of energy per day and once they were exhausted, they were exhausted.

This analogy can be incredibly helpful in describing how grief similarly affects energy.

The Spoon Theory

If you only had 12 'spoons' per day, how would you use them?
Take away 1 spoon if you didn't sleep well last night, forgot to take your meds,
or skipped a meal. Take away 4 spoons if you have a cold.

get out of bed   bathe   make & eat a meal   go to work

get dressed   style hair   make plans & socialise   go shopping

take pills   surf the internet   light housework   go to the doctor

watch TV   read/study   drive somewhere   exercise

The Spoon Theory was created by Christine Miserando.
You can find out more on her website www.butyoudontlooksick.com.

If you have only 12 spoons or units of energy per day, you consciously decide how best to spend them.

You may find it helpful to make a mental note each evening of how many 'spoons' you will need to get through the next day's tasks. Use this technique to ensure you are not overloaded or taking on too much and to prioritize the tasks which are most important to you, while not leaving you exhausted halfway through your day.

Be kind to yourself, listen to your body, and treat it with the love and respect it needs from you at this difficult time, and in return, your body will care for and support you too.

CHAPTER 2:

THE UNIQUENESS OF GRIEF

REQUIESCAT IN PACE

LIBBIE C. BAER

Cover with flowers the wound of the dart,
Fill it with flowers, the void in the heart;
Tenderest thoughts are unfolding to-day,
Sweet as the blossoms a-bloom in the May.

Think not of suffering, bloodshed and strife,
Think not of loss that hath come to thy life,
Think of the peace with suffering done,
Think of the glories their sacrifice won.

If you were to look for an explanation of the word 'grief,' the Merriam-Webster dictionary will tell you, somewhat unsurprisingly and rudimentarily, that it's "a deep and poignant distress caused by or as if by bereavement." True. However, what that meat-and-potatoes explanation doesn't express is the unmitigated and quintessentially unique way in which grief shows up for each person it visits.

David Kessler, best-selling author, renowned speaker, and grieving expert, views grief as being just as unique as each person's fingerprint.

David has further elaborated on how that uniqueness shows up in a common way for all explaining that no matter how each person grieves, everyone has a shared need for their grief to be witnessed. This is about needing someone to be there to see, hear, recognize, acknowledge, or feel their loss, what it means to them, and how it makes them feel, without trying to point out the silver lining or offer solutions or promises for the future. While it was once common for communities to gather together and to play an extended emotional and physical support role when a loved one has died, it's not so much the case in the breakneck speed of today's modern life. These days, our culture has a tendency to make the grieving person feel that while *their* life has been shattered, the rest of the world is carrying on as if nothing has changed. This can be a singularly alienating experience that reinforces the uniqueness of the pain of loss being endured as it appears that nobody truly 'gets it' or understands the depth of the loss being endured or how it has so radically changed the grieving person's world.

This incredibly unique and supremely individual reaction to loss affects people in a wide spectrum of both expected and suprising ways. It shows up in everything from exhaustion and an insatiable need to sleep to an inability to sleep at all. From a lack of appetite to increased appetite, particularly for 'comfort' foods. From a need to talk about how you feel to finding it impossible to talk about how you feel. From lethargy to manic activity and from numbness to abstract pain. The one thing that's certain is that your experience with grief is as unique as you are.

In those critical, final weeks before Dad finally rested peacefully, Mum had existed on cups of tea, takeaway cappuccinos, crackers, marmalade, meals kindly and generously provided by the nursing home, and sheer grit and willpower. More than that, she existed for every moment she shared with Dad. Sitting in a chair watching him for any minuscule flicker of need. At first encouraging him to eat and then, recognizing the anguish eating caused him, asking the staff to ease off and not try to cajole him to "just try one tiny bite," but to instead honor his wish to decide for himself. Gauging whether she needed to call the nurses for more medication to make Dad more comfortable or whether it was something she could help him with on her own. Watching TV with him. Showing him photos of his family. Saying his nighttime prayers with him, even after he had eventually stopped talking. Just sharing every precious moment together. As much as Mum so desperately wished for a miracle, for Dad to show signs of recovery and to come back home with her, back to the life they shared together, doting on each other day and night, she also knew that he had reached the point of no return.

The moment Dad was finally still, when he had breathed his last, when the pain, stress, and tortured, rasping anguish had all disappeared, leaving a calm but devastating silence in its wake, Mum's first thought was that her 'Bobby' was out of pain — there was no more suffering. But the void his passing opened up in her was immediate.

Mum was alone. Without her Bobby.

Gina, my tenderhearted and devoted sister, had spent years preparing herself for the loss of her father and had, in hindsight, somewhat naively believed she was well geared up to process the whole situation that was about to unfurl. She was left reeling in shock. She had not anticipated that he would pass away in the middle of a worldwide pandemic, which would prove to only add to the complexity of *what* we were dealing with and *how* we could deal with it. Her head was spinning as she was battered with conflicting reactions of nausea, heartache, disbelief, grief, and relief. She was drained, emotionally and physically, and yet was ready to offer her love and support to Mum and me.

Despite all her planning and preparation, Gina recalls the lead-up to his actual passing as being fraught with moments that ricocheted between holding her breath with fear, screaming with frustration, jumping out of her skin every time the phone rang in anticipation of the news it would bring, and clinging onto each other so tightly that her knuckles were white. But... also finding beauty, comfort, and love in the things that sur-rounded her and a newfound appreciation for nature. It was a perpetual source of solace in a time when she would normally be surrounded and upheld by the love and support of our extended family. She had to learn new ways of adapting to their support, albeit often on the doorstep or through a window, but certainly and sadly without the physical contact that would normally accompany the condolences of kind people, like great big bear hugs and the comfort of warm, safe arms surrounding her.

Ciara, my niece, a truly thoughtful, dedicated, and infinitely kind soul, who affectionately called HGLD, who was her granddad, Bobbyshafto, echoing an old children's nursery rhyme, was huddled there with us around Dad's bed, comforting him as he passed away. While she loved him dearly and will treasure the memories of using his belly and legs as a slide when she was just a poppet, she wanted him to find peace and to no longer be in pain so, for her, there was a sense of release. Ciara recalls looking at her Nana and feeling completely heartbroken for her. She was, as usual, most concerned for how everyone else was feeling and impacted by this life-altering event.

As for me, I distinctly recall how I felt the moment when Dad passed. It's a candid, high-definition emotional photograph captured and permanently locked into the heart of my mind and the mind of my heart. I was light-headed as I walked into the corridor outside Dad's room. The thoroughly disinfected light gray dappled linoleum floor had fallen away in front of me, like an earthquake swallowing up everything in its path, and somehow, the laws of gravity no longer applied in my Universe. Each step was a vertigo-induced moment of uncertainty. I didn't know how far down to place my feet to reach the ground. Everything around me seemed to be shifting upward, downward, sideward, or dramatically further than it should be as I moved. Nothing seemed real. It was confusing in ways that I didn't have words to describe which only served to make it even more confusing. Yet, it was also clear. *He was gone.*

In those weeks following Dad's death, I rallied together with Mum and Gina in an effort to slay the swirling emotional, physical, and paperwork storm and the long list of tasks to be settled (seriously, the paperwork!) on Dad's 'exit stage left.' We did our best to support each other, care for each other, and make progress, but also to make space for the grief which was slowly, silently, but surely making its presence felt.

We each wanted and needed different things at different times to maintain our balance, sanity, and ability to cope. Mum couldn't face going through Dad's clothes and other things but wanted it dealt with quickly so that particular fearful task wouldn't be lurking in his room, taunting her like a terrifying and ominous specter rising up and ready to consume. That, for her, was just too much. Not that she wanted it all gone, but she didn't want to have to go through that painful sorting and reminiscing exercise. She asked Gina and I to do it quietly when she was out of the house. We were also absolutely not ready to launch into that task, not yet. Not so suddenly. So, we kept putting it off. Buying time until eventually, a few weeks later, we couldn't put it off any longer. We knuckled down and spent an afternoon sorting Dad's innumerable shirts, cardigans, trousers, ties, scarves, and assorted paraphernalia into piles for each of us to keep as memories and piles to be given away to offer them new life and opportunity.

This exercise was a mixed bag for both Gina and me. Sorting through Dad's books, paperwork, clothes, and all kinds of assorted knickknacks and memories was a sweet and sour experience. It was heartening and heartbreaking at the same time. It felt like I was losing Dad all over again with every item I touched, held close, and sniffed to recapture the essence lost. Then there was the internal argument as to whether each article went in the 'keep' or 'to-go' pile, a decision that can be disproportionately torturous. But *not* going through Dad's things would have been a form of paralysis and fear that I knew would only grow and multiply. To deny myself this task would be to deny the joy, and yes, pain, of beautiful memories and stories relived through all my five senses. Memories of his cardigans, mints found in pockets, obscure notes in the margins of favorite books. Ah, the treasures to be found.

As difficult and emotionally fueled as that exercise was, I found myself reminiscing endlessly and happily about how Dad would so carefully select which shirt and tie to wear every morning. How he loved to match his scarf to them in the colder months. How, in his later years, he would pull the thermal hats down over his ears to feel snuggly warm. And many other wonderful gems of our shared history.

Eventually, after Gina and I had settled as much of the legal and practical aftermath as possible to ensure Mum had no confusing paperwork to worry about, we knew it was time for each of us to return home. Time for us all to begin a tough, unwanted journey of acceptance, reality, loss, pain, aching love, and grief in our own ways, on our own time, and on our own terms. We each needed to acclimatize to our new normal, without Dad. So, we packed up our cars and traveled in our small but deeply connected convoy of two on the 5th of December, 2020. Trundling our way from the lush, verdant midlands of Ireland down through farmlands, towns, and familiar sights, with heavy hearts and teary eyes to the ferry port in Rosslare and on toward home.

Even at that point, I didn't realize the true depth, breadth, and spectrum of my grief had not yet kicked in. I hadn't fully embraced that our family cornerstone was gone, missing from, and irreplaceable in our physical daily lives. Yet each of us who Dad had left behind — Mum, Gina, Ciara, me, and so many others who knew and loved him — had a rainbow of deeply personal responses to their loss. Every person was riding their unique gamut of emotions.

This highly customized, complex, and unpredictable journey of grief can, for many, feel like adding insult to injury. You may have at times wondered: "Why can't it just be predictable so I know what to expect? How long will this last? Or how far I am into or on my way out of this emotional roller coaster?" The reality is that every single person's experience of grief is like a carefully and delicately crafted snowflake; no two are the same. Grief, therefore, is the ultimate level of personalization.

This completely personalized journey of losing and grieving for a loved one is, as with all our life lessons, whether wanted or unwanted, there for a reason. However, that reason can remain shrouded and unclear until we are ready to understand it. It lurks hidden and so deep undercover that it might stump even the famous inspector Colombo. If only Colombo were here to help us investigate our grief, put it all together, package it up neatly, wrap it in a bow, and give us that clarity and resolution we need to feel better. If only, indeed.

Despite the desperately longed-for reversal of events and the unanswered pleas and prayers for things to have turned out so differently, we are where we are. In this soupy, thick, engulfing swamp of pain, sorrow, lethargy, foggy-minded sleepiness, regret, and hopelessness. Those rippling emotions were followed by hope, then another dash of hopelessness, doubt, aching and consuming love, and confusing uncertainty, or worse still... the certainty that *they are gone*.

While the wholly individual nature of our grief can make us feel like nobody hears, sees, or understands us, it is actually God's, nature's, or even The Universe's way (depending on your unique beliefs) of allowing us to feel what WE need to feel rather than having to conform to a 'type' of grieving during such an incredibly unbalancing, unsettling, uncertain time in our lives.

Yes, indeed, we have been gifted free will, making each of us, much like our journey through grief, a distinctly unique snowflake. Not the modern Urban Dictionary™ explanation of the adjective — wimpy or highly sensitive — but making us each unique, individual, and special. Honoring our divine right and need to be us.

As I wound my way through my journey of grief, so many things struck me as significant. Some are fleeting musings; others get stored away to be unpacked and pondered before being neatly tidied away for their next visit and exploration in my mind. Some of these ponderings make me smile, while others elicit a deep and non-negotiable sadness that demands my time and attention.

Loss and grief are not only different for everyone but are in fact different for each person in each experience they have with loss. I have lost people I loved before; my mother's twin sister, Tilda, who had fought long, hard, and bravely against cancer, my quiet and intelligent grandfather Matt, my father's younger brother Michael, and my Nana, who was the beating heart of our large extended family. But nothing had prepared me for losing HGLD. Losing *HGLD* was loss at an entirely different and life-altering level. The difference this time for me was that in losing HGLD, I had lost one of the greatest loves of my life; the irreplaceable love of a doting father, mentor, and cheerleader who had been so deeply connected to me for nearly 50 years.

What I now realize is... *there can only be grief where there is great love.*

The gaping chasm carved out in our lives when we lose someone we love dearly is not a vacuum; it gets filled with our grief. It's a rite of passage, a transition, or a bridge to carry us when we are ready to move on from *what was* to *what will be*. It's there to allow us time and space to feel what we feel until we are ready for the next step forward in our new reality. Grief has a role, a job, a vital place in our lives, and all the courage required to see that through. To get us through the most jarring and difficult stages of our loss.

When I feel the tears gathering up their skirts gracefully, ready to take their bow down my cheeks, I remind myself that my grief comes from love, great love, lasting love, and immediately I realize the truth in those simple words. I am grieving the loss of my HGLD, my Dad, and I know that I am grieving because of the love I had for him, shared with him, and still feel for him. I remind myself that I was blessed with that love and grew from that love. To me, it's worth the cost. I now understand with a clarity that is enlightening and consoling that in grieving him, I am honoring the relationship we have shared for nearly 50 years. I now understand that:

Grief is the ultimate celebration of great love.

Close your eyes for a moment and let that sink in. Feel the truth of it in your gut. Really, close your eyes, breathe it in.

We cannot grieve what we don't love. Most frequently, our grief is for the loss of someone we love greatly. This book focuses on that kind of great love. However, sometimes and very unfortunately, our grief is for the love that was withheld or simply and selfishly wasn't shown. The love that you were wishing and waiting for, hoping for and deserved, and now can never be shown as *they* are gone.

Grief is the unavoidable cost of doing business with love. It's the tax payable for experiencing love, connection, and affection which are some of the most basic human needs. It's fair to say that a tax is never fun to pay. Nevertheless, it's a tax that's *worth* paying because of how our lives have been so uplifted, enhanced by, and filled with meaning because of and through that shared love. I know I was incredibly lucky to have shared a huge, life-giving, confidence-building, golden-sunray-warming-you-to-the-depths-of-your-soul, heartbreaking love with HGLD, and my grief is the price of experiencing such love.

You may also, through your grief, be experiencing the price of the great love you had for your special someone. How you are feeling, whether it's swirling, achingly deep emotions, a lack of emotions, or even a void of emptiness, this is proof of not only how special and wonderful the love between you was and is, but it's also a testament to *your* loving nature and the love that you created. Your innate ability to love and to be loved is one of your greatest and most healing strengths, even at those times when it doesn't feel like a strength.

As you read on through the chapters, be sure to acknowledge the uniqueness of your love and your grief and take time doing the exercises at the end of each one. In doing this, you will develop your very own personalized guide to help you through your grief and to lead you to the comforting and resilience-building knowledge that..... the *Love Remains*.

How did it get so late so soon?

It's night before it's afternoon.

December is here before it's June.

My goodness how the time has flewn.

How did it get so late so soon?

DR SEUSS

BABY STEPS

Now that you have gotten to know HGLD, my Handsome God-Like Dad, a little, I trust that you can understand why I, as his adoring youngest daughter, came up with such a title to reflect the stars I had in my eyes for him. It was my fun but sincere way to explain how much he meant to me.

Let's lighten the mood and do a comforting and enjoyable exercise that will help you come up with your own meaningful and sincere acronym to express your love and feelings for the person you are missing and wishing was still here with you right now.

You can take the letters I choose for my Dad, HGLD, and find endearing words that are meaningful to you about your loved one, or form your very own acronym by choosing letters that highlight a fitting description for them. I'll get you started with some possible words, but you can be as creative, specific, and individual as your relationship with and love for them was.

Use this template and see what you come up with. You might even find multiple options, so choose your favorite.

Create your personalized HGLD acronym:

H	G	L	D
Some suggestions:	*Some suggestions:*	*Some suggestions:*	*Some suggestions:*
Happy, Herculean, Hearty, Hardheaded, Handy, Heroic, Heavenly, Honorable, Humble, Hot, Hypnotic, Humorous, Half-full...	Giggling, Gangly, Giant, Gentle, Gallant, Gaga, Gastronomic, Generous, Gentle, Genuine, Giddy, Girlish, Giving, Gigantic...	Love, Lover, Loving, Loveable, Lauded, Laughing, Likable, Learned, Leisurely, Leggy, Leader, Like, Light, Libelous, Loony, Loyal...	Darling, Dazzling, Daft, Dear, Dainty, Dancing, Dashing, Dapper, Dauntless, Deep, Debonair, Deeply, Defiant, Delightful, Disarming...

Or, freestyle it — the whole alphabet is your oyster:

Having your very own, very personal acronym for your loved one is an intimate and brilliant way to hold onto and instantly bring to mind all the wonderful things they meant to you and the special bond you had with your departed loved one. This can be your private alternative name, or you can share it out loud, bold, and proud. It will certainly be an interesting reference point offering you the opportunity to highlight some of their particularly special awesomeness.

You might just surprise yourself with the connection and comfort this simple task provides.

As we move on, you will notice that I sometimes use 'HGLD' throughout the book and especially in the *Baby Steps* exercises as an example, reference, or collective name for *your* loved one. Each time I use HGLD, know that it represents all our departed loved ones, not just mine, and most importantly, it symbolizes the loved one you have lost. In those circumstances, be sure to keep your special someone in mind and fill your heart with the unique attributes you chose through this exercise that fueled the love and relationship you built together.

CHAPTER 3:

GRIEF IS A STEALTHY COMPANION

GRIEF IN ME

JB OWEN

I know I was born to be me
To become all that I can be
And yet along the way
I felt betrayed
My mind went stray
My emotions frayed
I was lost in grief

Someone I loved, abandoned me
They died and although they were set free
I was left down on one knee
Fallen like a toppled tree
Unable to barely breathe
Not at all feeling like me

I cried, I raged, and screamed in pain
Their exit felt like pouring rain
Drenching my heart
Ripping me apart
Weakening my spirit like a poisonous dart

The me I knew felt less than me
My future robbed of what could be
My essence bobbed in a raging sea
All I could do was grieve
Lost and maimed in the broken me
Desperately wanting a new way to be
Begging grief to let go of me
So I could return to a happier me

A t a basic level, don't you think it's utterly extraordinary that every single person's experience with grief is different, individual, uncharted? One part of me thinks, well, yes, of course, it's obvious because we are all individuals. We have, to debatable and varying degrees, free will. We each have our own personalities. Our own likes, dislikes, beliefs, faiths, habits, inner dialogue, dreams, goals, hearts, minds, experiences, fingerprints, DNA, and even favorite ice cream flavours. A part of me ponders why going through grief can't be more like taking a test. You study, put in the hours, answer the questions, get enough correct to pass, and, "Hey Presto!" you are done. Through the grief tunnel. If only it was so black-and-white.

The singularly unique nature of grief, like the fabled coat of many colors, is something Charlene Ray, a Grief Wisdom Guide based in Washington State, USA, understands only too well. Charlene has worked with adults and children who have suffered the sudden and traumatic or long and slow loss of a loved one, whether they were a parent, spouse, sibling, child, friend, or coworker. With over 35 years of experience, in Charlene's own words, "There has been a lot of loss and a lot of grief to sit with." She has also had a front-row seat having lost her father when she was only 13, her grandmother at 25, her mother at 49, and her brother when she was 56. Not to mention losing several close friends and beloved animal companions along the way. Grief has deeply informed how Charlene works with and helps others.

Often when people seek Charlene out, they are in shock, disbelief, and have the sense that what has happened to them is all a bad dream.

Many struggle to function in day-to-day life and experience physical symptoms such as exhaustion, aches, and pains. While their initial emotions are sometimes numbed, which is a very frequent reaction, the inevitable sadness comes quickly, along with a whole spectrum of feelings that become their very own emotional coat of many colors. Charlene has shared a great deal of her experience as a Grief Wisdom Guide with me, and through this book, I will share some of the insights she has gathered from her years of working closely with people struggling through their grief. Many of her observations and her wisdom will undoubtedly strike a chord with you.

In fact, I have a collection of wonderful individuals who have 'been through the wringer' of grief and have either made peace with their loss or are on the road to achieving balance in how they experience their grief and live their life after loss. I will introduce you to them now so as we proceed through their experiences, you can begin to feel less alone, more connected, and certain that, despite your loss and grief... *Love Remains*.

I have a wonderful friend, Esther, who is undoubtedly one of the strongest people I have ever known. Esther and her fiancé Matt had been together for 12 years. They had a lovely house, a gorgeous puppy, and were looking forward to their wedding, which was just a few months away. Like most couples, they had some 'hiccups' along the way, but they were happy, positive, and excited about their future together.

Having developed flu-like symptoms over Christmas, Matt woke up the day after Christmas struggling to breathe and a day later was in intensive care in the hospital. Instructions were quickly and solemnly issued to gather his family there immediately. A week later, in what felt to Esther like the blink of an eye, he had astonishingly died of staphylococcal sepsis at the much too young age of 35.

Esther was in absolute shock, confusion, and disbelief. She didn't understand what had just happened. Had he breathed in something that had killed him? Just like that? It made no sense. And suddenly, the soon-to-be bride's world had turned upside down. Esther found herself in a surreal reality where Matt was, with virtually no warning, missing from everyday life and everything they shared as a couple. Being the strong, independent woman of action that she is, Esther found the reserve to keep functioning and doing the things she needed to do. Just without the man she planned to marry. For her, the loss was felt so deeply in knowing, seeing, and feeling that he wasn't there. Not in their lovely home. Not on the planet. Just so immediately and irrevocably.... gone.

Let me introduce you to Pat Labez. Pat is quite simply one of the most upbeat, positive, and joy-filled people you will ever come across. She is one of life's inspirational souls who keeps those around her moving forward, smiling, and feeling great. Her upbeat nature has not excluded Pat from joining the grief club. Pat and her sister Joy were very close. Joy was number seven and Pat number nine in a large and loving family of nine siblings. Joy had a big heart that was shielded by a serious front, and she somehow found herself in the matriarch role of the family, taking care of their parents' needs as they aged. She didn't marry but enjoyed playing Auntie Joy to nine nephews and two nieces, including Pat's daughter Amanda Joy. In December 2012, Joy was diagnosed with stage IV pancreatic cancer and stage II breast cancer. The pancreatic cancer came with the devastating news that it was inoperable. Joy was told she had between one and three months to live and was advised to get her affairs in order. But Joy was determined to fight, and Pat was equally determined to support her in every way possible, including researching treatment options and different cancer centers. Pat, through a friend, came across a new redox signaling cellular health supplement and added it, with Joy's permission but without mentioning to the medical team, to Joy's medication regimen.

To everyone's surprise and delight, Joy immediately responded positively to the treatment. Her oncology team called her their miracle girl. It was at this point that Pat told them about the supplement to which the doctor said, "Whatever you're doing, keep doing it." Joy continued to improve, and everyone around her started tentatively picking up their lives again, while keeping a watchful eye on her.

Then, some three and a half years later, Joy's health once again declined. Despite the preparation that came with the cancer diagnosis and what appeared to all who loved this woman so much to be imminent, there was still an overwhelming sense of disbelief. The last six months were truly difficult. Joy, Pat, and all their family and friends were simply physically, emotionally, and mentally exhausted. Joy loved life, but those final months were not life as she knew it to be. There was nothing more Pat or the medical team could do to avert or change the course she was on. For Joy and Pat, it was time to accept God's will. That also brought with it a deep sense of relief. Pat was Joy's constant companion in her final days, playing Hawaiian and gospel music, just as she wished.

Joy took her last breath as the words to a favorite song played, "Let me walk through paradise with you Lord. Take my hand and lead me there." Then, peace, comfort, no more pain, and no more sadness.

For Pat, it was a turning point. A critical, transformational learning. Life can be fleeting. Her new mantra became: "*Carpe diem*, seize the day!" Pat hadn't known what a bucket list was until Joy mentioned it, but they had managed to check off a few items on it, including New Year's Eve at Times Square, New York. It was magical. Now Pat doesn't take anything for granted but embraces whatever is in front of her, whether it's new and exciting or daunting opportunities, experiences, relationships, freedom, and particularly, her health. Pat now embraces life with great gusto and passion.

Every single path of and through grief is unique. It's real. It's a personal path. And since you are reading this book, it is likely a path you are on, and I am here for *you*. No matter how you are experiencing your grief... just know... *you are doing it exactly right* for you.

This necessarily unique journey has shown itself to be a cunning beast of many faces after the loss of Dad, my HGLD. Those of us closest to him, despite the signs doled out along the fated expedition of his final months, weeks, days, minutes, and breaths were blindsided, dazed, and winded by the vast suddenness of it. I was unreservedly, wholly, and absolutely stunned into my grief.

Family, friends, and neighbors reached out to share their profound sympathy and condolences. They offered help. They called. Texted. Sent flowers. Then called some more. And watched vigilantly for any discernible falter so they could be of some help to us.

At times of great loss, people mean well. We know that. They offer a much-needed *dash of supporting loved ones through their loss.* Sometimes they say kind, sweet, thoughtful, gentle, caring things in the hope of conveying, all too often supremely clunkily, their support. Still, it can, at times, make us want to scream, smash something, run for the hills, or hide away and not answer the door or the phone.

We hear, "It'll take time," or, "'In time you will feel better," when it feels like nothing will ever again, in any distant figment of our imagination, feel better. Often we don't even *want* to feel better because that might imply that it's okay, that we have moved on and everything is normal again. That can be too much, too far a stretch for our grief-addled imagination.

While "It'll take time" can sound so basic, trite, unaware, and perhaps even a smidge dismissive of the gravity of our loss, there is some truth to what they say. Yes, it will clearly take time and somewhere inside of us, we know that. It's just that we can't find the fast-forward button to get to that magical pain-free place in the future. And yes, it will, with time, become more bearable, less consuming, and, dare I say, easier. It's just that from where we are, floored, caught, trapped in that sticky web of grief, we are too close to the burning core of it to have space for perspective or logic.

Ah, perspective! What a magnificent gift bestowed in greater magnitude to those on the outside of grief than to those who really need it on the inside. It's a little like when we were young and first fell in love with the boy or girl from next door or school. The innocent kind of love which fell apart to what felt like devastating consequences when we heard he or she went to the movies with someone else. It felt like the world had ended. Stopped. Nothing would ever be the same again. That we would never, ever love again. Our parents and friends would try to comfort us and say that we would get over them in time. It really didn't feel like we would, but of course, they were right. We did. Perspective. So much easier on the outside of pain. All we were missing was *a generous serving of clarity and understanding.*

However, these well-intended ladlefuls of advice from others can also make one feel that they are not heard, not understood, that they are not doing grief right, or that they must be so thoroughly broken, more broken than anyone else because otherwise what they are hearing would make sense or feel more right than it does.

HGLD lived to be 79. But, if I had a dollar for every person I have heard say, "Well, he had a good innings!" I would be able to make a nice dona-tion with it to the Alzheimer Society of Ireland. As I smile back at the well-intending person, inside I am questioning why on earth don't they realize that 79 was far too soon to go? Can't they hear how dismissive they sound? I wasn't ready to let him go. Funny though, before losing HGLD, I am pretty sure I said the same thing to others who had lost a loved one at a similar age. I certainly didn't mean any disrespect or to play down their loss. But, when on the receiving end, it feels like they just don't understand. Perhaps that's because they don't and that's not their fault. It's okay for them not to understand. It means they probably haven't yet lost someone so near and dear to them.

Particularly in the early days and weeks after loss, many want to tell you how sad they are that your special someone has died. It's comforting to know they were appreciated and lovely to hear how they are so fondly remembered. These family members, friends, and acquaintances have also shared memories, stories, love, and a desperate need to share this with you. Sometimes, they want and need to cry on your shoulder so you find yourself doing your very best not to cry. You let *them* pour it out. You thank *them* for their kindness. You end up supporting and consoling *them*. This sympathetic shoulder you offer to others, despite your intense loss, is a little kindness you give back to those who loved your special someone also.

The good news (good news because it means you are, contrary to your own opinion or doubts, doing this grief thing right for you) and also the bad news is that it's not all meant to make us feel good. Some things we see, hear, smell, taste, and touch will inevitably bring our loved ones immediately to mind. Some memories will bring back moments of happiness, even joy, sometimes just for a fleeting moment. Other times it will linger longer like a heady perfume, wafting around us. The constant echoes of your loved one can also herald the ceaseless onslaught of stinging tears and impassioned pleas to whatever higher force you believe in to return them to you — that you will do anything, anything at all for one more minute with them.

This compendium of feelings is your right. More than that, they are your stepping stones through this deeply personal journey.

But it's important to realize that you don't have to be held hostage to the well-intended advice or comments of others. When you feel that you don't want to be cajoled along, cheered up, fixed, told an anthology of stories about others who have died or are grieving, advised or otherwise pestered by ill-timed, infinite, or exhausting, albeit good intentions, it's crucial to get people to just *listen to you*. To sense what *you* want, not what they think you need. To be willing to be quiet with you or to carry on as normal around you rather than constantly hovering, asking if you are okay, telling you how great you are doing or what you need to do. Ask. Use your words. Be kind but firm. It's not only okay to do this, it will help your friends and family know what you want and how they need to show up for you. Remind them when they slip back into the muddy waters of overzealous advice that the greatest gift they can give you is to listen.

It can be difficult at times, or perhaps more so with particular people, to explain your need for them to listen more and talk less. However, for many, this self-protection action sidles into the territory of confrontation, and if you are already struggling with your grief, the thought of having a potentially difficult conversation with someone may be simply too much. If that is the case for you, if you are worried about offending anyone, or, when put on the spot, if you just can't muster the energy or words to explain how you are feeling and what support you really need, you could consider creating your own sign or note to explain it to them. You may find this an easier way to be heard, and your helpful friend or family member will probably be relieved to know how they can be of most support to you. There is a *Baby Steps* exercise at the end of this chapter to help you with this.

> *"When you talk, you are only repeating what you already know. But if you listen, you may learn something new."*
>
> DALAI LAMA

On the flip side of excessive input and advice from others, you may also have been surprised at the absence of some of your closest confidants. One or two people you had expected to be checking in on you have, after some perfunctory expressions of condolence, vanished into thin air. People simply don't know what to say or how to help, are so afraid of saying the wrong thing, or just feel useless or impotent. Subsequently, they back off. Radio silence. Tumbleweeds.

While this can make you question their friendship, it's likely more a reflection of them not knowing what to do to help. Again, in this case, the stalemate smasher can be you proactively asking them for help. Whatever help you need. It might be to cook a meal, collect the children from school, meet you for a coffee or walk, sit with you to keep you company, or be there to listen. Help them to know how to support and help you. They will undoubtedly be glad that you have reached out and given them the option to be of use.

Esther was very aware that some people might be uncomfortable talking with her about Matt's death and would worry about saying the wrong thing. To help them out of this minefield, she explained that she was equally okay with talking or not talking about Matt and answering any questions they might have. However, when one particularly good friend of hers went AWOL for several months, Esther asked her why she had been distant. Her friend confessed that she just didn't know what to say.

For Ciara, sadly, losing her grandfather, her Bobbyshafto, was not her first foray into loss. Shortly after she turned 17, Tom, one of her best friends, someone she was beginning to form a romantic relationship with, became a tragically young victim of suicide. On receiving the shattering news from her best friend over the phone, Ciara fled in a daze down the stairs of the family home so fast that her mother, my sister, thought she had fallen. She couldn't breathe and could feel her heart beating mercilessly in her throat. Her thoughts made no sense, and she was covered in a rash brought on immediately from the shock. Wrapped in her mother's arms, clinging on tightly, the news seemed impossible to take in.

After losing Tom, Ciara found it incredibly hard to come to terms with the fact that she wouldn't see him again. She had so many questions she wanted to ask him. Questions for which the answers would never come. She began to struggle to communicate with others. That internal turmoil, which silenced her and held her emotionally captive, lasted for many months. She felt anger toward anyone she spoke to because the only person she actually wanted to speak with was Tom. That resulted in her becoming uncharacteristically introverted and starting a pattern of going straight up to her bedroom after school and crying herself to sleep, feeling so alone and unable to express or resolve what she was feeling. Ciara's not sure how long that lasted but, to her, it felt like a lifetime.

You see, we human beings are a tribal species. For thousands of years, this tribal instinct has protected and provided for us physically and emotionally. It has enabled and ensured our very existence. The ultimate intuitive instinct within us is for survival, and this driving impulse developed our need to connect with others, to build and work within our tribe. As you step along the uncertain path of your grief, now more than ever you need connection with those who make you feel safe. The people you can lean on.

The support of people you trust, particularly once you help them know what support you need from them, will bolster you and hold you carefully as you inch your way through the various stages of grief to come. I have often reminded myself that many of these family members and friends have endured their own devastating losses. This left me more receptive and respectful as they offered us the benefit of their *experience helping others overcome their greatest traumas.*

The process of grief is for many, though certainly not all, an unavoidable, frustrating, painful, agonizing, hurtful, limiting, and crushing experience. Yet it can also be a patient, helpful, fortifying, and necessary way to regain balance and transition into the next phase of our life. Until we reconcile ourselves with the implications of this loss, until we reach a point of acceptance and realize that alas, there is no 'do-over' and that we are, whether we want to or not, embarking on a new phase in our own lives. But until we let that in, we remain in a kind of holding pattern of feeling lost, scared, daunted, bereft, and broken. Until we reach a point of acknowledgement of what has happened, how it affects us, and decide how we want and are willing to proceed, we may remain on the not-so-merry-go-round arguing and fighting back against something we have no control over.

You may already have heard of the Five Stages of Grief, a pattern of adjustment as described by noted Swiss American psychiatrist Elisabeth Kübler-Ross first in her iconic 1969 publication *On Death and Dying* and later in her 2005 publication *On Grief and Grieving.* You may even have referred to it before, either wittingly or unwittingly, when talking to or about others who have lost someone close. My oh my, but it's so much easier when it's about someone else to see the rationale, to have perspective. Don't you think?

As useful and reflective as the model is, it is equally vastly simplified when considered theoretically and superficially in comparison to the nitty-gritty reality we endure when stuck inside it, like going around and around in a spin-dryer. Grief doesn't always happen in such a neat, tidy, and predictable flow. Frustratingly it's rarely so clearly defined and linear. In reality, grief is disjointed, awkward, annoying, devastating, recurring, abrupt, iterative, immediate, gut-wrenching, out-of-order, and not unlike a meerkat, popping its head up, constantly making you feel you are in an exhausting and never-ending game of Whac-A-Mole™. It's a hungry, devouring, and insistent cycle which is actually much maligned and misunderstood in its purpose, like the grim reaper himself. He gets a bad rap as an evil omen who has come to cut someone's life short and steal them away. In reality, he's more like the liaison officer sent to escort one at the point of death to their next phase.

The stages of grief are a kind of 'Groundhog Day,' constantly replay-ing and in a different order, over and over again, waiting with infinite patience for our active acknowledgment in order to proceed. It's there just tolerantly waiting, quietly whispering, "It's okay, take your time. I can wait." No menace intended, just eons of patience while we fight with the inevitable.

This is a game of 'who blinks first' and, my friends, grief wins every time. It's a cycle that can be prolonged for many by our need to continuously disagree with, challenge, or fight it; imagining somewhat misguidedly that we can influence the outcome... an outcome that has already been reached and written in stone. We want a time travel machine to go back and fix it, to change the past. What I wouldn't give for a DeLorean™ with a 'flux-capacitor' and some plutonium right about now. But that's only possible in the movies.

Sometimes we skip a stage entirely and are left confused and thinking, or being told, that we are getting it wrong. Thoughts run around our heads in endless circles; not only did we fail to keep our loved one around but we are even failing at grieving properly!

Let's take a moment to get to grips with the traditional stages of grief as outlined by Elisabeth Kübler-Ross.

Denial: It didn't really happen. It can't be true. When I wake up, it will all go back to normal. Like me, thinking: "But he was just here, he was alive a minute ago." If we were to open the floodgates to all the feelings of loss at one time, it would simply be too much to deal with. Denial and shock help us to cope when overwhelmed.

Anger: It's my fault — I didn't do enough. Why didn't he look after himself better? The doctor was negligent or at best neglectful. He didn't fight hard enough, long enough. How could he leave me here? The anger doesn't have to be logical. That's almost the point of this phase. An outlet. Another tool to protect us and stop us from crumbling. Anger shows us that we are still alive. We still have breath and energy. Interestingly, the anger hits once we realize, on some level, that we will probably survive whatever comes.

Bargaining: If you give him back to me, I will be a better person. Just one more minute with him and I will do anything you ask. This phase can kick in before or even after bereavement, making us desperate to influence the inevitable and impending ripping apart to come. Desperation. The notion that there is a higher power that will right the wrong and give us a second chance if we can just identify the price of the "favor." I know that I would have happily sold my heart, soul, and breath to take away Dad's pain and suffering. Strange then that the higher power did indeed take away his pain and suffering, without me having to sell my soul. Just not the way I had wanted. Still, the right outcome for Dad; pain and suffering extinguished. Forever.

Depression: My whole reason to live is gone. I can't go on. I don't even want to. I have no purpose to live. Depression is a quiet form of desperation. It feels like there is no point in forming words anymore because nobody gets it, nobody understands, and nothing can make it better. I am broken, unfixable. Lost. But these heavy and overwhelming feelings of depression when grieving are normal. They are how our nervous system protects itself by shutting down and giving us time to adapt. This kind of depression after loss should not be mistaken for clinical depression, for which one should seek appropriate help.

Acceptance: Not to be confused with being okay with what's happened, this is more about surrendering. Very few people are ever okay with losing a loved one. Acceptance is often seen as the final stage when people accept that their loved one is gone and will not come back. However, for many this is a springboard right back to other phases that have not yet been sufficiently aired, like Anger and Depression. But, this phase exposes the first glimpse of light at the end of the all-consuming grief tunnel. The more focus is spent on Acceptance, the more we are gradually recognizing that day-to-day life is still going on. We still have to shower, dress, brush our teeth, eat, work, exercise, sleep, and get up and do it all over again. It's not like life was before, it's altered, but life somehow is going on.

The mistake is to assume that in order to exit grief, we should no longer miss them, cry, or not think about them every day and be good with it. We expect to be somehow lobotomized so we don't talk, think, or feel our loss. That's neither reasonable nor desirable. To no longer miss them would be to no longer remember them or take joy and comfort in the time you had together. It would mean to forget them. Perfectly unreasonable, undesirable, and wholly undoable.

The Five Stages of Grief — *Denial, Anger, Bargaining, Depression, and Acceptance* — are, for many, the flexible framework through which we work our way toward learning to live with our loss. They also go a long way toward explaining why, at times, we feel the way we feel; angry, sad, frustrated, desperate, lonely, overwhelmed, empty, numb, hurt, and all the other confounding, swirling, and happiness-crushing emotions. Understanding and, to some degree, expecting the stages of grief can help us in a number of ways. That help can come in the form of acknowledging and giving permission to feel the emotions as they hit us, recognizing that what we are feeling and going through is typical and to be expected, or offering a 'time-out' from our anticipatory grief and a more balanced emotional state.

Throughout this emotional roller coaster not only do we feel all these conflicting, unsettling, and confusing feelings, but when one looks deeper, dives down another layer, underneath and underpinning these feelings are neurological changes taking place in the brain, which affect emotional regulation, memory, multitasking, organization, and learning.

When grieving, our bodies become host to a rush of neurochemicals and hormones. Some of the most common ways these pesky critters make their presence felt are by disturbed sleep, loss of appetite, lack of focus, ruminating, confusion, forgetfulness, fatigue, anxiety, and depression. This is often referred to as 'Brain Fog' or 'Grief Brain Fog.'

The upside of this flood of neurochemicals and hormones is that they are your body's way of caring for you. They make you slow down, switching off the intense multitasking and high energy we might be more accustomed to in our grief-free existence. The body's objective in doing this is to give us time and space to adapt. To gradually work toward Acceptance and reengage back into life.

For many, stress is intricately stitched into the lace of grief. Stress from the desire for an outcome other than the one we are faced with. Stress from the tangible, financial, practical, emotional, and physical changes. Stress from fear. Fear of the *unknown* and fear of the *known*. All this stress releases the hormone cortisol into the bloodstream, particularly in the first six months following loss. Cortisol directs attention away from nonessential body systems during a fight-or-flight response, and it affects our immune, digestive, and reproductive systems all in an effort to ensure critical systems remain functioning as it senses danger is imminent. Generally, once the perceived threat has passed, hormone levels regulate and return to normal. That perceived threat can repeatedly raise its head as we make our way through the five phases of grief, waiting for us to reach Acceptance, the signal that we will be okay. We can handle this. *You can handle this.*

For a small number of people stress, of loss even results in the temporary heart condition takotsubo cardiomyopathy, also known as broken heart syndrome. According to Harvard Medical School, takotsubo cardiomyopathy is a weakening of the left ventricle, the heart's main pumping chamber, usually resulting from severe emotional or physical stress, such as a sudden illness or the loss of a loved one. That's why the condition is also called stress-induced cardiomyopathy, or broken heart syndrome. So appropriately named.

Therefore, when you feel exhausted, unable to focus, forgetful, foggy, and find yourself feeling low and just wanting to close your eyes and sleep indefinitely, it's important to know that this is normal. It's a common response to exactly the situation you find yourself in. Your body is looking after your needs at a time when you perhaps aren't.

This is a time to rest your mind and body. Give it what it's asking for. That doesn't mean you should hide under the covers and do nothing but perhaps, just for a while, step away from incessantly vacuuming the house or constantly mowing the lawn. Fresh air, gentle exercise, healthy balanced meals, rest, and the willing ear of the friend all play a key role in your physical and mental well-being. Avoid making major decisions until you know you are free of the fog. Be kind and loving to yourself. Begin to console yourself the way you would console someone you care greatly for.

We are, each of us, experts at being us. But we are not experts at finding our hesitant way through this grieving process. This is new, uncharted, and filled with uncertainty. We are even less expert at helping our other loved ones, our family, and friends, who are also grieving the same loss but in their way. We feel what *we* feel, not what *they* feel. We each do what helps us to survive, whether that means talking, not talking, reaching out or not, locking ourselves away quietly, or pushing outward to smother the quiet internal whispers of ache with activity and words and connecting with friends and family.

It's highly unlikely that we are the only ones who are suffering this loss. Certainly in the case of losing Dad, I know that not only Mum and Gina are intensely and irrevocably affected, but there are many other close family members and friends sharing in his loss. While we can do whatever possible to help those in pain around us, we shouldn't take on the full mantle of managing others' grief. We bring our car to a mechanic when a service is due. We call a qualified electrician to fix the wiring and a plumber when we spring a leak. We should equally seek the help of experts and open the door to qualified grief counselors, support groups, and online support and books to help ourselves and our loved ones deal with our loss in a way that feels right for *them*.

There is no perfect way to grieve. My way is not the right way for my sister or mother. Theirs is not the right way for me. Sometimes the best thing you can do to protect and support yourself and others is to bring in the pros to help them the way *they* need. Experienced professionals who can listen without an agenda; who have tools and approaches we haven't even considered but which might just make a world of difference.

We can perhaps feel the mistaken responsibility to make everyone around us happy and comfortable, console them, and be strong for them. That's fine in normal life. Yes, be strong, be someone others can depend on and even look up to. But right now, in grief, it's time to allow yourself to feel your feelings. As sure as night follows day, the feelings will remain there circling under the ice, waiting for it to thaw so they can be released.

And when we do allow those feelings to have space, to find their voice, we find ourselves on the way toward Acceptance, finding our balance and inner strength. This is the beginning of feeling and cherishing the love that remains.

"Well, everyone can master a grief

but he that has it."

WILLIAM SHAKESPEARE

BABY STEPS

Your grief is *your* unique journey. *Your* personal expression of dealing with the loss of your loved one. Sometimes it's quiet, other times it has a thundering voice. For some, it comes with tears, for others not so much. However you are feeling and dealing with it, it is your right, and you only need your own permission to do it your way, in your time.

1. Flash-forward in time — My advice to my current-day self:

Have you ever found that it's so much easier to give sage and balanced advice to others who need help than it is to know what to do to regain *your* footing when you are in the eye of your own storm? When it's someone you are helping, you can perhaps see and understand their situation and what they need with greater perspective than they can as they are too close to the situation. Think back when you gave advice to a friend or family member who was going through a difficult time. You probably found a gentle, loving, and confidence-building way to show them the path through their situation or at least to help reinforce that they would get through it. Even if you haven't had the opportunity to help advise someone else, you might have been on the receiving end of similar wisdom or counsel and found, once through the storm, their more distanced perspective to be both true and helpful.

Now, it's time to give yourself the same perspective that you have offered others in the past.

Imagine you are at some point in the future when you are back to feeling more like you again. Stronger, happier, more able to do the things you want to be able to do. A point of time in the future when you feel capable, balanced, and, while you still miss your loved one, you are living life with joy once more.

Doing this will help you to paint a picture of the future that you want and deserve and what it will take to get you there. If you find it difficult to write your letter, imagine you are writing to someone else who is in your situation. Someone you care greatly about who is struggling with their grief. Someone who trusts you and needs you to help them through.

Think about how you would sincerely and truthfully inspire hope in someone else and capture those words, knowing they will offer the love, comfort, and perspective that is missing for that person as they weather the storm.

It's time to put pen to paper. Write a letter as that older, wiser you to the you of today, focusing on how to advise and help the younger grieving you, and above all, inspire strength and hope for the future.

Example:

Date: September 12th, 2021

Dear Younger Me,

I am so sorry that you are struggling with the loss of _____. I know how much it hurts you. I understand how it overwhelms you when you least expect it, grabs hold, and makes you feel _____.
I know the fears you have and the doubts they have, at times, poured into your life.

I know you. The real you. Nobody knows you better than me. I will always be truthful with you and will always have your back because I am the you who has survived this.

So, there are some things I need to share with you.

Firstly, you survive this.

You are stronger and more resilient than you know.

It's okay to feel sad and to cry.

It's also okay to feel lighter and happy.

You did everything you could and should have done.

While you will always miss_____, it does get easier.

You have happier days ahead. Really.

You need to take time to allow yourself to grieve.

You are doing this right.

But when you know you have rounded the corner, it will be time to take action and throw yourself back into life again.

Don't avoid rounding the corner. Whether you do or don't affects your happiness. Luckily, I know that you *do go* round the corner.

You made _____ very proud.

You make me very proud.

I need you to know these things because they are true. For now, though, take your time and talk to yourself with love and respect. Be kind to yourself. When the time is right, be firm and brave. I know what you are capable of!

Your life is waiting for you, and you have so much yet to do. I am there waiting for you with open arms.

Love,

ME, age xx

Now, write your letter to the grieving you:

Date:

Dear Younger Me,

Now that you have written the letter from the older you, who has survived grief, to the younger you of today, who needs to know that you can and will get through this intact, allow at least a part of you to be open to the wisdom and perspective that has come from this experience, in your own unique way and in your own time.

2. Well-intended advice of others

I have found it incredibly helpful, not just while in grief but generally, to calibrate what I think someone is trying to say to me with what I hear and, most importantly, what they actually mean.

Doing this can help put yourself in the other person's shoes and imagine you are outside of the situation, rather than inside it. Therefore, you aren't experiencing it in the same very personal way as the person on the receiving end of the well-intended advice. You might also be able to think back to times when you offered someone else guidance when they were going through a difficult time.

Use this template to get to the true and well-intended meaning of what people are trying to say when they offer you advice about managing your loss, how they think you should grieve, or what they think you should do, keeping in mind that generally others truly want the best for you.

Doing this exercise will offer you a more true and balanced perspective of what others are really trying to say and how they are trying to help. This will also remind you that you are in control of your own choices about what you believe and what you do. That feeling of being in control will offer you a boost of liberation and empowerment.

Well-intended advice of others	What they actually mean or want for me	What I choose to believe or do
Example: Time is a great healer.	I'm so sorry you are hurting. I wish I could help. It must be really hard. I want you to be ok.	I miss him/her so much but I am resilient, I am stronger than I feel, and I am a survivor.

Now when someone says something to you that makes you feel frustrated, unheard, or unseen, you can refer back to this exercise or even take a moment in your mind to work it through from what they said to what they *really* meant and then to what you *choose* to believe or do.

3. Helping others to be better listeners

It's not always easy to ask people to be better listeners. Particularly the friends and family who unquestionably mean well and have your best interests at heart but who are perhaps a tad strong-willed and effusive in their support. Feeling like you are always being told what to do and how to grieve can be an energy drain you can really do without, particularly when much of your energy is being directed like a life-support system toward keeping your head above water and managing your grief. Yes, you know they mean well and want to help you. So help them to help you better. Now is the time to be clear about how you want and need their support.

It can be difficult to think of what to say when put on the spot. A useful technique to help manage this situation is to write out what you want to say to strong-willed yet caring people.

An alternative is to use that same information and create a small note you can give them. If you decide on this approach, it's important not to enter into a discussion about it. Just give them the note, perhaps with a hug, and leave it at that. It's okay for you to need things done your way at the moment.

Sharing your feelings with a note will allow the receiver to understand what you need from them and how you want them to show up. That will, in turn, diffuse the awkwardness they feel when they want to help but either don't quite know how or, alternatively, when they try to force you down an unwanted path of their choosing only to be faced with your resistance. For many, notes like this are an effective way to gently set necessary boundaries without debate, which can be difficult for both sides.

Create your note here and include any of the suggestions from the example that you feel relate to you.

Example:

Thank you for caring about me the way you do. I love and appreciate you very much, and I'd like to ask for your support during this difficult time.

I am grieving an incredible loss in my life and am doing my best as I move into the next phase without _____. I am feeling over-whelmed by the continued advice and direction I am receiving from so many people.

What I need and what will help me most is for you to listen when I feel like talking, to be quiet with me when I feel like being quiet, to chat about anything else other than my loss, to chat about it when I am ready, to go for an occasional walk or coffee, but not to offer advice or try to fix anything unless I seek advice.

I am incredibly grateful for your understanding, kindness, and friendship.

_____

_____

_____

_____

_____

_____

_____

_____

_____

Once you have composed your note, be sure to give it to your friend or family member in a manner that helps them understand their support is important and valuable to you. This might be with a hug, in a thank-you card or letter, or perhaps along with a gentle smile.

Doing these exercises will help you gently and gradually, in your own time, build back up the control which you may feel, through your loss and grief, has disappeared. Sometimes you won't feel like doing the exercise. Sometimes the anticipation of doing it will feel overwhelming. That's so often the way when trying anything new. Just take your time, don't rush, but don't skip over them either. See each exercise as a gift you are giving yourself and that's exactly what they will be. These *Baby Steps* will become your friends and your strength as you move forward through the book and your life. You *deserve* this. You *can* do this.

CHAPTER 4:

THE UNSEEN MONSTERS

TIME IS KIND

DR RAOLEE

Someone said to me...
Time, time is kind
In different sorts of ways
Time heals the wound
No matter how deep it cuts
Time mends a heart
That's been broken into bits
Time eases the pain
No matter how much it hurts
Time dulls an ache
That's been nagging for so long
Time ceases the tears
No matter how much you cry
Time fades the anger
That is burning in your mind
Time, time is kind
To the sad and broken hearts
Many things are said
On how kind time can be
So I smile and I know
That with all the support
Time will be kind to me.

The loss of a cherished person from your day-to-day life can undoubtedly have far-reaching, supremely stubborn, often invisible yet enduring ramifications. I call these the *Unseen Monsters*. Why? If you are grieving someone incredibly special and important to you, the *Monsters* bit is pretty obvious. *Unseen* because, for those of us left behind in the queasy, grabbing, rocky wake of loss, most of what we struggle to deal with is quietly hidden in our thoughts. It's the inner dialogue that drips fearful and at times deeply unsettling words through the silence. It tricks us into being so certain that coping, overcoming, or moving on is frankly impossible and 'clearly' out of the question. The fear that comes with grief can be intangible and difficult to pin down, understand, or communicate. You may not feel like this all the time. Some days will be better than others. Some days you feel stronger, more positive, and not so consumed by the ravenous *Unseen Monsters* that underpin your grief. Other days, they linger like an unwelcome life-sucking force preventing you from believing that you can and will survive this. You *can* survive this loss. You *will* survive it. You have already proven yourself to be a survivor, to be strong. The only permission you need to survive the emotional turmoil of grief is your own.

Let's look at the first *Unseen Monster*, the sense of disconnection. Previously, in Chapter 3, we considered how we humans are a tribal species. How connecting with others has, since men battled with woolly mammoths, provided safety and security. We are to a great extent driven by this basic natural instinct to connect. To seek out connections that make us feel good, allow us to be seen and heard, to find solutions to problems, to laugh and to cry with, to feel valued and wanted. When a pivotal central force in your life has been swept away, that feeling of being left adrift, uncertain, and alone without that beloved someone can easily and often result in feeling disconnected. While you have, at least in the daily physical sense, been disconnected from that vital person, the sense of disconnection can spread like a virus ravaging through your body and mind, making you believe, feel, and act generally disconnected.

This *Unseen Monster* of disconnection multiplies, grows, and bears down on us when we begin to feel and then reinforce with our thoughts and words that, "Nobody understands my pain." It's like life is trying to carry on all around you as normal. How dare life continue so casually, unfazed and unruffled!

In order to sidestep that disconnection and change your doubt-ridden inner dialogue into something much more loving and empowering, allow me to share some fundamentals about how the mind works.

A little known but life-changing truth is that your mind will always do what it thinks you want it to do. In fact, your mind receives its instruction and programming from your thoughts and words. Not the things that others say to you or do to you but what *you* choose to let in from those interactions. In practical terms, what this means is that everything you think and say is accepted by your mind as what you want, and then your mind jumps into action to make it happen. For example, if you were to say or think to yourself repeatedly, "I'm terrified of spiders," you will find you are indeed terrified of spiders. If you were to say or think to yourself while exercising in the gym, right at the point when you feel you can't do anymore, "Just one more set of lunges, then I will stop," you will find that you can probably squeeze out that extra set of lunges.

> *"In our thoughts and words we create our own weaknesses and our own strengths."*
>
> BETTY EADIE

Another truth about how your mind operates is that it is primordially motivated to protect by directing you away from pain and toward pleasure and safety. This means that anything you link with pain, for example talking about your loss, sorting through the personal items they left behind, dealing with the paperwork and legalities, getting out of the house, accepting invitations, or thinking about continuing on and planning a life without your special someone will feel particularly tough. Your mind will go to great lengths to drive you away from any notion of participating in any of the activities you link with pain. With this same intention to protect you, anything you start to link with pleasure or safety, such as not going out, not having to deal with conversations and the inquiries of others, perhaps even not bothering with getting dressed into 'outside' clothes, or existing on tea and biscuits (if even that) rather than healthy balanced meals, the mind will encourage without hesitation.

In its mission to give you what you want based on what it hears you say, to keep you from pain, and give you the pleasure and safety you seek, the mind gets busy, prompting you to pull away from others to avoid the pain you have associated with those connections. Your mind hears your inside voice crying out, "Nobody understands my pain! Nobody gets it! Nobody has ever felt this agony or loved the way I have loved!" As a direct result, you might begin to withdraw, disconnect, isolate yourself, and perhaps also resent outside interference, all because your mind is following the direction of *your own words*. Meanwhile, the well-intending interferers see their inquiries and offers of help as being caring and supportive. You, on the other hand, might begin to dodge phone calls, entirely ignore that your wardrobe contains anything other than pajamas, sweatpants, and T-shirts with holes in them, or stop answering the door, going out, and keeping up with your usual activities. All because these perceived dangers risk putting you with people you believe don't understand what you are going through and bombard you with their caring advice.

Many struggle with how the death of their loved one impacts aspects of their identity. Herein lies another lurking *Unseen Monster*. As a Grief Wisdom Guide, Charlene has seen each of her clients go through a phase of questioning. Questioning who they are without this person. Wondering how their identity has changed and who they will be going forward. Esther has talked about how before Matt died, she had a clear path ahead of her and knew how amazing it would be; marriage, with children, and enjoying happiness. Then, suddenly that clarity, that path had been blown up like in an explosion. With no direction, no path, Esther felt lost, alone, and confused.

Mum's world had irrevocably been turned upside down. She was alone. Without her Bobby. The exhaustion of the preceding months hit like a hammer. The truth of this new reality was barely conceivable to her. Immediately she missed her Bobby with every cell in her body. A physical and emotional pain like no other. She misses seeing him on the sofa. Misses the chats, catching up with friends and making new friends in the local cafés together, watching their favorite TV programs, making cups of tea for each other. His voice. Laughing until their sides hurt over silly, simple things. His smile. Just knowing he's there. The purpose to her every day. And suddenly, with the snuffing out of his shining light, everything Mum knew, understood, and enjoyed about her daily life was no more.

Change of this magnitude is hard and can leave one questioning their very identity, their understanding of who and what they are without the person they miss so much. Seeds of doubt can be planted in these tumultuous times as our powerful internal voice raises shake-you-to-the-core questions and statements like, "Who am I without _____?" or "I can't do this alone." This internal questioning can make us feel small, scared, broken, alone, and fearful of what the loss of this person means to our life and identity. While it may sound counterintuitive, this negative self-talk is a protective though futile technique that our minds employ in a last-ditch effort to hold onto what 'was' and to resist what 'is.'

When someone we love so profoundly disappears, it leaves a huge gaping, aching hole in our hearts, minds, emotions, plans, and lives. All those times when you would turn to them to share your news, a joke, a smile, or a tender moment, seek advice, comfort, understanding, and consolation, you can't turn to them anymore. At least not in the same physical sense as before. Perhaps no one ever worried for you, cared for you, or got you like them. When they are gone, the world seems unsafe, and our life is forever altered. Realizing that the intense pain of grief is the price of great love, our instinct to avoid pain can push us away from going down that road again.

It can feel frightening. Scary. Real. Tangible. Immovable. Overwhelming.

Consuming. And yet, it's *invisible*. And life is carrying on around you making the experience all the more detaching. This is the reality of the *Unseen Monsters* that accompany grief. However, this is the reality that the words, shared experiences, and Baby Steps in this book will help you turn into something much more powerful, empowering, loving, and doable.

Another of those *Unseen Monsters* is good old-fashioned guilt. From my own first-hand experience, I can confirm that guilt is a slippery vortex that pulls you down and holds you in the past, asking yourself all kinds of senseless, destructive, and unanswerable questions. What could or should I have done differently to stop this from happening, to prevent them from dying? Was I a good mother/father/daughter/son/sibling/partner/friend? Did I show up for them like I should have? We worry away like a dog protectively focused on gnawing and grinding down a huge bone at all the missed opportunities to show them we loved and cared for them. We worry if we did enough to help them, make their lives easier and happier, and make sure they felt connected and valued. We torture ourselves with these looping, panicked, guilt-ridden thoughts like a lab rat stuck in an endless and exitless maze. Guilt is like a cruel experiment being monitored by some unseen higher force, testing us, evaluating, making notes, endlessly watching the rat run panicked with no hope of salvation.

The result? Rarely anything good or productive. Rather, we become unfocused, disinterested, numbed, forgetful, tired, and lethargic all the time, unable to get enough sleep or get to sleep at all. We lose our appetite or begin to comfort eat, as if that food can push down the swelling emotions.

Ciara found that guilt was one of the hardest emotional responses for her to manage. She would constantly badger herself like a determined prosecuting attorney asking what she could have said or done differently. Although she knew on a logical level that she wasn't responsible for Tom's death, it took her years to believe and accept it. Even 10 years later, she still occasionally, through her silent thoughts, asks Tom why he did it, still seeking answers to the unanswerable.

Sometimes, we don't even want people to talk to us. We don't want them to cheer us up, we don't want to have to engage and respond to them. We don't want them to rob us of even a moment of our intense loss and grief, a delicate gossamer thread we cling to in our desperation to maintain our connection with our loved one.

These *Unseen Monsters*, the fear, loneliness, questioning, doubting, lamenting, the feeling of being broken and unfixable, frequently come with a side order of long bouts of uncontrollable crying or even the inability to cry. It's a pain that we fully understand is emotional, but stranger still is the physical pain that rears its ugly head. Pain with a spectrum that runs from a dull ache all the way through to acutely feeling like you just can't stand it anymore. We feel this physical pain in part because grief is felt in the pain center of our brain in exactly the same way as a physical injury. This is an important key to help dial the distress and confusion back down. Understanding something gives you power and control. Understand that when you feel all these feelings, both emotional and physical, it's your mind and body doing their job to listen to and protect you. To prevent you from venturing into situations that could hurt you and, instead, to give you the time and space to come to terms with this transition in life.

Esther developed some brilliant and imaginative techniques to pull herself out of her lowest moments, the times when her *Unseen Monsters* dared to take over. At those times, she would ponder what could be worse than what she was going through that others have had to face and came up with a whole bunch of pretty awful things. This comparison to other people's difficult situations gave her perspective in the moments when she needed it most. When she found herself welling up with tears while talking to people but didn't actually want to cry, she would divert her energy, attention, and emotions by going through, quietly in her own mind, all the ingredients that go into a typical English 'fry-up' breakfast — "Fried sausages, grilled bacon, fried tomato, fried egg, sauteed mushrooms, baked beans...." The novel aspect of this was that Esther doesn't even particularly like the typical weekend breakfast treat of an English fry-up. But it frequently had the desired outcome in stopping her tears from brimming over. Distraction and activity are some of our best friends at this time. *One cup of the generously shared experience of others.*

Challenging and changing our long-held belief systems in the wake of grief is another example of an *Unseen Monster.* For Ciara, Tom's passing was the straw that broke the camel's back in terms of her belief system. Having been raised in the Catholic faith, she had begun to question some of the ideologies surrounding organized religion as a young teenager. But when Tom died, these questions were promoted from theoretical musings to a deeply emotional reaction. Suddenly, she found it impossible to be around churches or any places of worship. When her beloved Bobbyshafto passed, Ciara was 26. This time losing a loved one had entirely different repercussions. This time it made her feel closer to religion than she ever had since she was a child. She attributes her different reaction partly to being in Ireland at the time of her grandfather's death, where she found the faith others embraced to be undeniably uplifting.

When Dad passed, Gina recalls thinking, while we were plotting a course through the necessary arrangements, changes, and stresses over the following weeks and months, that we — Mum, Gina, and I — were doing well, all things considered. But now, as she looks back with a little time, distance, and perspective from those exceedingly emotionally raw days, she can see it would have been easier to cope and process what was going on if we each had our 'rocks' to lean on. She was missing her husband, daughter, and friends. I was missing my partner, daughter, and friends. Mum needed her siblings, extended family, and close network of friends. We craved physical contact with those we loved and depended on. But COVID-19 had intervened and put a stop to that. Instead, we leaned on each other, resulting in three devastated and bereaved women clinging to each other.

Weathering the tsunami of grief, while held in its engulfing swells yet attempting to function, to get stuff done, to put on a show of being okay, brings to mind the trusty comparison of being a swan. Graceful, calm, strong, 'together' on the surface but with the feet peddling frantically out of sight. You may identify, either in your grief or in other stressful times, with that swan and the *Unseen Monster* of carrying on regardless. Paddling frantically, keeping your head above water.

Despite the onslaught of your *Unseen Monsters*, now is the time to allow yourself to feel what you are feeling. To recognize that what you are feeling is okay. It's truthful, sincere, and, like all feelings you have had all throughout your life, it is transient in nature. Deep feelings, whether happy or sad, can be remarkably like a spinning top. They start with vast intensity of force and speed, with a momentum that appears infinite. But, gradually, they lose pace, reduce energy, and fizzle out into a more balanced, realistic, stronger, happier state. Over time. Not overnight.

Though it might not feel like it, this turmoil and complexity in how you are feeling shall pass. As frustrating, far-fetched, and flippant as this sounds when on the receiving end of this pearl of wisdom... it's also the one thing that, as I review my personal history and the grief experiences others have shared with me, consistently turns out to be true. In fact, everything you and I have ever struggled with (exams, jobs, relationships, arguments...) all passed, and we moved on from them.

But, while stuck there in the muddy depths, there might just be a part of us that doesn't want that deceptively wise adage to be true. A part of us that is resisting reaching the Acceptance stage because we have misunderstood Acceptance as being good with our loss. And so, some throw themselves fully, absolutely, and wantonly onto the sword of grief and begin defining their life by the grief they are in.

While it may feel dauntingly impossible that the exhausting anesthesia of grief will ever lift, it does. It changes, it passes, it becomes something entirely different. Something kinder and more manageable. Something that gives strength and a lightness which ignites a knowing smile to reflect the memories and the love we hold inside.

When the people we love disappear, who we are and what we are doesn't disappear with them.

You have already proven that you are a survivor. Consider this carefully. Let those words in. You have survived everything life has thrown at you so far. You were born with incredible survival skills. You are, without a doubt, already thoroughly tested and have proven yourself to be unbreakable. Now that is something to take comfort from and to celebrate.

"One of the greatest discoveries a man makes,

one of his great surprises,

is to find he can do what he was afraid he couldn't do."

HENRY FORD

BABY STEPS

Now that you understand how your mind seeks clarity and direction from your thoughts and words, you understand the powerful influence your words, whether the quiet 'inside' words or the out loud ones, have over your reality.

When we seize control of our thoughts and words, we bring about an incredible shift in our decisions, our habits of action and beliefs, and ultimately, our feelings.

1. Seizing control of my thoughts and words:

Seizing control of our thoughts and words is all about learning to talk to and about ourselves the way we would talk to or about someone we love or respect greatly. It all starts with choosing better words and doing it consistently until your mind believes you. For many talking to themselves in a loving and supportive way is a brand new muscle to create and exercise.

Here's what to do:

1. Use the left side of the template to make note of the hurtful, harmful, unsupportive words and thoughts which are building hurtful, harmful, and unsupportive beliefs, habits, and feelings. These are the things you hear yourself think, say, or perhaps even do which make you unhappy or bring you down.

2. Then, for each of the hurtful beliefs you have listed, on the right side, capture kind, caring, supportive, strengthening, and loving words which you would use to establish new kind, caring, supportive, strengthening, and loving beliefs. It's okay if you don't yet believe or feel them; you are going to build that muscle by using those words. It's important here to only describe what you *want* rather than what you want to stop feeling or happening.

3. If you are struggling to find nice things for the right side, think about what you would say to support someone else you care greatly for.

4. Choose to stop saying the hurtful things on the left. When you hear them pop into your head or come out of your mouth, choose to say, "That's not me. I don't say that anymore."

5. Choose to be kind to yourself. Start saying the new words from the right side all the time. Start by reading them to yourself from the list (only the right side!) 10-12 times each day and do it without counterbalancing those wonderful words and thoughts with any notion of not feeling or believing it yet or that it's not true. You are only now starting to program them into your brilliant mind, and it needs clarity and consistency. The beliefs and the feelings that match the words *will* follow.

Example:

Old outdated hurtful, harmful, unsupportive words, thoughts, and beliefs	New words to create new kind, caring, supportive, strengthening, and loving beliefs *(what you want, not what you don't want)*
I am alone	I am blessed to have family and friends who care and support me I am resilient and am doing brilliantly, HGLD would be so proud of me
I feel broken	I am strong I am getting stronger every day
I can't cope	I have amazing coping skills I know how to love and care for myself

Now, add yours:

Old outdated hurtful, harmful, unsupportive words, thoughts, and beliefs	New words to create new kind, caring, supportive, strengthening, and loving beliefs *(what you want, not what you don't want)*

Old outdated hurtful, harmful, unsupportive words, thoughts, and beliefs	New words to create new kind, caring, supportive, strengthening, and loving beliefs *(what you want, not what you don't want)*

When you consciously choose your words carefully and begin to talk to yourself with great care, love, and respect, you open up the possibility of and the pathway toward Acceptance and resilience.

2. Take time to acknowledge how I feel

One of the primary causes of depression is the suppression of our feelings. It has been said that, "The sorrow which has no vent in tears may make other organs weep" (Henry Maudsley, 1835-1918, pioneering English psychiatrist).

Take a little time to find the words that describe how you feel. This is an exercise you can keep coming back to as new feelings arise which you find difficult to understand or explain.

I feel....	Because....	And now....
Examples: Lost, adrift, and alone — nothing is secure or permanent	HGLD was there all my life and now he's gone	I will focus on the relationships and people I still have and treasure those blessings; I am not alone
Relieved for HGLD and for us	It was really difficult to watch him in pain and distress that nobody could fix; he is free of pain now	I am human with human reactions, it's okay to feel this way, this is normal and natural
Guilty	I should have done more or found a way to save him	I know there was nothing more I could have done, I wouldn't want him to feel guilty if our roles were reversed, I will be kinder to myself and honor his wishes

I feel....	Because....	And now....

By doing this exercise you will find, over time, that putting words to your feelings and giving them time and space to exist can provide great comfort, understanding, and acceptance within yourself.

CHAPTER 5:

WHAT I MISS ABOUT HGLD

THE WINDOW

RUMI

Your body is away from me
but there is a window open
from my heart to yours.
From this window, like the moon
I keep sending news secretly.

When someone we love so dearly has passed and we can no longer just phone or video call them for a chat, drop over for a cup of tea, see them across the dinner table, consult them for advice, or sit with them for quiet and understanding company, very often what pulls us into grief is the loss. Loss of their company, voice, kindness, laugh, wisdom, and so many other things that made us feel connected, reassured, and happy.

But, grief isn't only about looking back into the past. It can also be hitched to the loss of hopes and dreams for the future. Hopes and dreams such as things we had looked forward to and planned to do together but now cannot. Things that we will miss sharing, having, and doing with our someone special. This is the painful double whammy of missing what *was* and missing what we thought *would be*.

The 'missing' feeling we experience in grief can be a tricky and unmapped minefield, giving rise to feelings of betrayal (how could they leave me like this?), guilt (at the prospect of continuing with the plans we thought we would share with them), or anger (I didn't sign up to be left alone to do all this!).

In spite of this, the ability to acknowledge what we miss about them also helps us to lay down a path toward Acceptance; that liberating sign above the exit door in the intricate foggy maze of confounding grief. The door beyond where we know the air will be sweeter, our bodies will feel lighter, energy will enliven our limbs, and somehow, life will go on. Altered, yes, but with the potential to begin to paint the canvas of our lives once more.

For many who are grieving the loss of someone special in their lives, what we most frequently miss are the love, friendship, companionship, shared experiences, their touch, hugs, smiles, smells, sounds, winks, support, and the balance they provided to our own occasionally skewed logic. But we also can miss the more practical things that our loved ones did for and with us, the role they played in our lives; arranging the finances, balancing the checkbook, cooking, gardening, tidying up, sharing their knowledge and special skills, researching the pros and cons when making a big purchase, fixing things, painting walls, being the driver, protector, guide, and map reader. So much to miss, but in all likelihood, that's why they were so lovable and vital in our lives. To not miss a loved one when they have passed is far too much to expect.

In order to feel Dad's presence around us, after he was cremated, we had tiny amounts of his ashes interred in small wooden heart urns, sometimes known as 'cuddle stones,' which are the size of the palm of your hand. Mum keeps one upstairs in her bedroom and another downstairs in the siting room, so she has Dad nearby. When she wakes up, she sees that heart and feels his presence. Every morning, as soon as Mum goes down the stairs, she wanders into Dad's room to say good morning to him, but the quiet stillness of his room evokes in her an unbearable loss. It reminds her of all she misses about him. Most of all, his fun side. He loved to make her laugh. Even right up to the months before he passed he would hide behind the sitting room door and peep out at her, then burst out laughing like a child. Mum still pictures him doing that. It's the simple things she misses most like giving him a hug and simply chatting or watching their favorite TV shows together.

If there was an award for the most sentimental person, I think it would go to my sister, Gina. She has always been deeply sentimental and, to this day, finds it a gargantuan struggle to ever get rid of anything as everything ties her to a vivid and loving memory. The list of sentimental aspects she misses about her 'Pappy,' as Gina often and lovingly referred to Dad, is happy-memory-inducingly extensive and includes his voice, laugh, smile, and hugs to how he would call her '*Pet Lamb*,' his terrible 'Dad jokes,' how he would crack us all up by modeling his pajamas complete with socks and everything all tucked in. She misses how he would stir his tea. The way he would sing and whistle *ALL* the time. The sheer delight on his face when he'd have ice cream, some crispy fried bacon, or a good burger. The joy he found in making us, as little girls, 'egg in a cup.' That he was all things Christmas. How smartly he would dress every single day. His infinite array of ties. Hearing him scrape the bottom of every bowl or plate — the man loved his food! Seeing him fastidiously and constantly folding and refolding napkins which was a 'thinking' habit. His stories. His walking stick and its myriad of uses. She misses just watching him glued to the television as he would avidly enjoy everything from documentaries to dramas. She misses seeing him walking around wrapped up in his zipped-up coat, scarf, hat, and gloves. She really misses being able to ask him for advice, holding his hand, his smell — always clean, fresh, and wafting one of his favorite aftershaves with every movement or tiny gust that gently kissed him. Just knowing he's there. So much to miss.

Pat misses the spur-of-the-moment 'just because' chats, the laughter, the adventures, travel, and hula dancing with her lovely sister Joy. You see, Joy was a master at getting people together and celebrating life, whether it was a birthday, holiday, a visitor, a win somewhere; no matter how small, she was gifted at finding a reason to celebrate and whipping everyone up in her particular brand of positive energy. Dearly missed.

Charlene, whose father died when she was only 13, has missed having a father in her life. She misses the way he loved and adored her. She misses talking to her mother and her sweet spirit every day. Her mother was the first person Charlene wanted to tell everything to and she still finds it hard not to be able to do that. She misses her monthly check-in phone calls with her brother and his sage advice, positivity, and encouragement. She misses her grandmother's support and love. So many things to miss but so many things that have enriched her life along the way.

For Esther, what she misses, all these years later, is just the fact that Matt isn't here. Sounds simple, basic, and obvious. But it's an unpluggable gap. She misses his great humor, friendship, companionship, and support.

Thanks to my bolstering and overflowing *cup of memories,* everyday I find myself reminded of a vast cornucopia of things I miss about my HGLD.

Things like how, some years ago during Mum and Dad's extended stays with me in England, when I would work from home and spend my day chairing back-to-back conference calls solving problems across the globe, he would listen in excitedly, letting his blood begin to percolate and rise to bubbling over like it did when he was the captain of his ship of factory workers not too long before. Like how he would take great pleasure at waking up early in the morning to drive me to the station to catch the 6.25 or even the 5.55 AM train, just for that five-minute car ride and chat together. Or how he would be there at the station patiently (always early) waiting for me on my return at 7.05 or 7.35 PM and often later. As soon as I would cross the threshold of the station exit, I would see his face light up with the excitement of a child on Christmas morning in anticipation of what stories he would skillfully and tenaciously extract from my day's adventures. How with a twinkle in his eye he would, with precision, begin his interrogation with, "So? Tell me everything, start at the very beginning... You walked in and said hello, then what?" How when he wasn't satisfied with the level of detail, he would jokingly suggest that I "Elucidate with diagrams where necessary." His breath would quicken, his eyes dance, and he would chortle in a way that would warm the very cockles of my heart as I regaled him with the happenings of the day. To him, it was no less exciting than being smack-dab in the middle of an Indiana Jones™ movie. Those short journeys to and from the local train station were his lifeblood. They were the greatest adrenaline rush of his day, and he savored every word and every moment. He would egg me on, always encouraging me to go for it, to use my head, heart, and voice to lead with conviction, and to make a difference through my work.

Some things invariably make me sad but others uplift, cheer me, and keep me connected to him. Some infuse great happiness into my day. More still remind me of how lucky I was and am to be his daughter and to have had nearly 50 years of a joint-life story that can never be erased or diminished.

As I think about all these 'missings,' what strikes me is how the things we miss about our loved ones have molded us into the people we are today and the choices we choose to make. It's crucial to realize that while our loved one may have gone, the things we miss about them continue to shape and benefit us.

These things we miss are the gifts that keep on giving. As I look back over my list of 'missings,' I see a vital, sparkling silver thread connecting HGLD's life, his philosophy, energy, beliefs, and habits, to mine. Not a carbon copy, not identical; we are all individuals after all. But the connection was baked into my DNA and further evolved through our shared life experiences making our connection both reassuring and undeniable. What is also undeniable is how those aspects of HGLD both shaped and *continue* to shape me as a person in addition to my choices.

Because of this 'baked in' effect, while we don't have them physically with us, we without a doubt have them always with us.

Missing *your* special someone may be very tough and may take time to get used to, but the aspects and memories of them that you miss are an impenetrable connection that cannot be lost or stolen. It's yours to keep, forever.

"The song has ended but the melody lingers on."

IRVING BERLIN

BABY STEPS

Capturing the things you miss about your loved one and tracing those aspects through to how they have shaped you as a person and your choices can be incredibly comforting, cathartic, and fortifying.

When I did this exercise, I found myself reminiscing with smiles, laughs, and overflowing gratitude for all the special moments I was so lucky to share with HGLD.

Things I miss about HGLD

- Sitting together in Dad's favorite restaurant in Windsor enjoying a burger, fried onion strings, banter-filled chat, and our undeniable closeness while Mum enjoyed a look around the shops.

- Fishing with him on Lough Corrib in the west of Ireland when I was a child, helping him to prep and push his little blue fiberglass boat out into the water and pretty much always coming back empty-handed but happy.

- Sharing our libraries of books, both of us relishing the frivolous fiction which would bring dashing characters like Alex Cross and Jack Reacher leaping off the page.

- Accompanying him as a young girl on regular journeys from Wexford to Dublin, using that time strategically to pester him with endless questions about his childhood.

- How he would laugh at his own incredibly silly jokes, which were rarely original or actually all that funny, but he would mine them for every minuscule grain of golden giggle dust.

- How, even when tired, he would happily join me in the car to buy a pint of milk, just for the opportunity for a chat, and from fear he would miss out on any excitement.

- How he would suit up with his coat zipped, buttons buttoned, snappers snapped, from top to toe, hat pulled snugly down over his ears, scarf always matching his tie, which was folded neatly around his neck and down his chest, gloves on, shoes shined, walking stick in hand, and book under his arm, standing by the front door 20 minutes before we ever had to leave the house telling us all we were going to be late.

- Seeing him mowing the lawn on his ride-on mower, loving the freedom and mobility that his legs had long since denied him. Almost as good as being a getaway driver from a bank heist in a movie!

- How he would love watching and feeding all the local birds or 'birdeens' as my Nana (Mum's Mum) would call the teeny-tiny little ones. This peaceful and heart-expanding activity would always make him feel close to Nana, who he adored.

- Seeing him enjoy a charred yet juicy inside steak with a 'mess' of fried onions or his favorite takeaway fried chicken when he would have extended holidays with me in England. Seriously, nobody could imagine the abstract pleasure that he got from the £4.50 meal. I don't think a Rolls Royce™ would have made him any happier.

- How he would make a 'mud pie' on his plate out of any meal which involved mashed potatoes, gravy, or a sauce of any kind. He would do this for my sister and me when we were little in a somewhat misguided effort to get us to eat up whatever vegetable we were artfully dodging.

- His constant encouragement, which would propel me forward in my career, buoyed up by the belief he instilled in me that I could achieve anything.

- How when my sister and I were little, he could make anything mundane feel like an adventure.

- How when either my sister or I was being gently reprimanded, he would refer to us as 'Luvvie.'

- The heady scent of his Fahrenheit™ aftershave, always liberally applied then lingering and wafting around him like a heavenly cloud.

- His inexhaustible positivity.

- His natural ability to rise above adversity of any shape, kind, or form.

- Seeing how fast his brain worked. It was like watching a sped-up ballet.

- His voice. Though I can hear that at any time I choose

Use this template to capture your special connections with *your* loved one. Remember all the times they made you laugh and the aspects of them that made you feel seen, heard, important, special, and loved. If you get stuck, look for sparks of inspiration from my list and see what it brings to mind.

Being specific in how you describe the things you miss about your loved one and how these things have shaped your life is a powerful way to focus on the positive aspects of your memories, rather than the sadness of 'missing.'

What I miss about them	How it has shaped me and my choices
Example: How he would sing all the time and make up the words as he went along	Taught me to choose to be happy, to find happiness in small things, and the powerful impact this can, in turn, have on someone else's day

Now that you have completed this exercise, use it to transform your sense of missing someone into a powerfully uplifting trip down memory lane. You can even make this part of your daily routine or a 'go-to' exercise for a boost of connection and comfort.

CHAPTER 6

WHAT I LOVE ABOUT HGLD

A ROBIN RED

GEORGINA MURDOCH-STONE

A loving glance, a watchful eye,
Herald Angels observe on High
With hands entwined, we whisper "Why?"
This gentle man must say goodbye.

But length of time, and love's embrace
Create the image of his face
That comforts us, in our quiet place
Helping guide us with his grace.

A year has passed, the 'firsts' have gone
And though we sometimes feel undone
We close our eyes and wait for dawn
And our memories will carry on.

A smile so bright, a look of love,
A robin red, a tiny dove,
A twinkling eye, a hand in glove,
Loves pure light sent from above.

doubt there are many who aren't acquainted with that frequently doled out oldie-but-goodie quote by Alfred Lord Tennyson, "It's better to have loved and lost than never to have loved at all." Despite the underlying truth, it's another of those wise-isms which is considerably easier to dispense than to receive. Which side of that particular love fence you fall on is a personal perspective. It's a glass half-full or half-empty choice. For me, to question whether it is better to have loved and lost is like asking if it's better to have breathed and lived or to have not breathed and not lived. Love, just like breath, is crucial to life. So yes, I most absolutely, positively, and unquestionably believe it is better to have loved.

It's the 'lost' bit that I would like to redefine. Choosing to see my *love* glass as half full, I unreservedly believe that the love I shared with HGLD is permanent and comes with a lifetime guarantee. It remains with and inside me. It's mine to keep, hold onto, enjoy, reminisce, grow from, and celebrate. When I need consolation or reassurance, I just add *one overflowing cup of love* and let it absorb.

When chatting with friends and family members about Dad, they invariably and very quickly shift into divulging the fun stories of times and adventures they shared together. They effortlessly recount the things they love about him, how he impacted their lives, and what he meant to them. Rather than making me sad or lamentful, these conversations from the heart lift me and make me so proud.

In Charlene's experience of working for many years with clients who are grieving, she frequently finds recurring themes with regard to what they loved and considerable crossover between what they loved and what they miss about their special someone. Primarily they talk about loving wisdom, advice, and personality traits such as their kindness, caring, and compassionate nature. When it comes to what Charlene loves about those whom she has lost along the cobblestone path of her own life, it's her father's sense of humor and desire to really enjoy life. She loves how her mother was so kind and thoughtful, that her brother was the most encouraging person she knew, and how her grandmother loved her unconditionally and was always there for her as a child.

When Pat Labez thinks about what she loves most about her dearly missed sister Joy, it's her spirit and thoughtfulness and how Joy would notice even the little things in life. Joy's outlook on life has helped Pat to embrace that same vitality and spirit, opening her up to seeing the beauty all around her and to participating in life in an entirely new and more energized way than ever before.

Esther, being such a bright, positive, and 'can-do' person, was strongly attracted to many similar characteristics in Matt. She loved his humor and how silly and fun he was to be around. His passion for music and culture, which often ended up being more of an obsession, for example, a particular album or a theater show like *The Phantom of the Opera* or *Les Miserables*. His love of cooking. That he was willing and able to talk about things and work through any difficulties with Esther meant the world to her. Because of this, they rarely argued, both preferring to either come to an agreement or to agree to disagree. She loved that he got on well with her brother. That he was in touch with his feminine side. She loved how he would encourage her at the weekends to stop, sit down, and relax — something that, while necessary, doesn't come naturally to her. Quite simply, Esther loved that she always felt safe with Matt.

Mum loved and still loves Dad "to bits" and "everything about him." In particular, she loves his kindness and how patient he was with her, only ever wanting to see her happy. This resulted in her feeling totally loved and cared for. She still feels cared for as she feels him close by all the time, carrying Dad in her heart and talking to him constantly. The one thing that helps her to feel calm when in distress is to place her arms around the beautiful polished wooden casket containing his ashes. With that hug and that contact, she suddenly feels calm and able to cope. The *Love Remains*.

For Gina, it's so easy to roll off a litany of the things she loves about her Pappy. Many are the same things she misses, which makes sense.

His laugh, smile, dress sense, and scent. How he loved our mother. His love for his daughters and granddaughters, Ciara and Simone. How he could relate to his sons-in-law, Ian and Simon. His bonds forged with the wider family and dearly loved friends. How, though each person was different, he could still form a connection with them. His cheeky, wicked sense of humor. His bravery in the face of extremely challenging and deteriorating health conditions. The way he looked at our mother with complete and unconditional love. His devotion to all things Christmas. His business acumen and vast knowledge of almost any subject. The constant love he had for a mother he had no recollection of, except for a few photographs. His unceasing love for nature, particularly dogs and birds. How wonderful that the fragrance of these things lingers with us, indefinitely encouraging, comforting, cheering, and warming us to the core.

While I know that HGLD is gone in the physical sense, in a much more powerful and enduring way, he will *never* be gone. Because of the time, experiences, and love we shared, he will remain with me always.

However, this kind of positive thinking is not wishful thinking or mumbo jumbo, it's not woo-woo or only for those who meditate. It goes so much deeper in the physiological sense.

When we think about love, we tend to immediately link it to the heart, but the brain is actually where all the real action happens. For example, in the first flush of love, when we feel excitement and great pleasure at the very thought of seeing or spending time with our new love, the brain emits the 'feel-good' neurotransmitter, dopamine, which is associated with pleasure and reward. Dopamine continues to be released; as we reinforce our positive connections with that person, whether romantic, familial, or platonic. Another key chemical linked to love is oxytocin, which develops feelings of attachment, safety, and trust. Oxytocin really comes into its own after that first flush of love, supporting longer-term connections, earning it the well-deserved moniker 'the love hormone.' These and other neurotransmitters and hormones, such as endorphins and serotonin, which are increased through exercise and a healthy diet, all work to regulate mood, reduce stress, and increase positivity and general well-being.

All meaning that *now* is the perfect time for us to focus on the transformational power of love.

Undeniably, love is a major contributing factor in the connection that you shared with your loved one and how that connection shaped, comforted, and empowered you. It's no surprise that love is known as the emotion that makes the world go round. It's also the emotion that, through the release of dopamine, oxytocin, serotonin, and endorphins, gives you the courage to make brave choices. Those brave choices are fueled by feeling more positive, strong, and capable within yourself and more connected to those you love and care for. As you focus on love, whether it's the love of the people in your life or the love of what you enjoy doing such as exercising, cooking, reading, walking in the park, feeding the birds, or decorating your house, it opens your heart up to the transformational healing, soothing salve of love.

Love can be found in the little things, the common things such as smiles, twinkling eyes, a caring touch, or simply time spent together, as well as the special, unique, and distinctly memorable things we share and enjoy along life's journey. These things you love are like tattoos on your heart, there to stay, to keep, and to enjoy all through life.

When I think about HGLD, it's exceedingly easy and extraordinarily pleasurable to not only remember but to reignite deep inside what I love about him. I feel it's important to clarify that these are not things I loved about him; this is not past tense. I can give myself this gift of love at any time, anywhere, and as a result, provide myself with a much-needed breath of fresh air, lift, smile, or laugh.

As you read through my list, I encourage you to think about what *you* love about your special someone. Dig deep, and you will recall the special, quirky, and distinctive aspects that drew you to them, that connected you to them, and that you can tap into at any time to feel that love, comfort, and unique connection again. There is an exercise at the end of this chapter in the *Baby Steps* to help you capture the things you love.

What I love about HGLD

- His twinkling eyes

- How he would crack himself up telling the same jokes or stories over and over

- That he would take my sister and me on 'magical mystery tours'

- How he would let me snuggle up with him in the big swivel chair to watch our favorite programs on TV

- Christmas dinner was an extravaganza of which he was King

- That he loved everything about Christmas and embraced it like a child; festive movies, music, Christmas trees in every room, lights, and decorations everywhere

- How he loved animals and they loved him

- The wondrous, far-fetched yet enthralling stories he would spin for us as children

- His natural and unconquerable positive 'can-do' attitude and habits

- His amazing intelligence both learned from the subject matter and human behavior

- His love of beautiful music

- How he would conduct music as he drove

- His ability to make up ridiculous and hilarious words to songs when he didn't know what they were

- His boarding school stories of escapades with friends like raiding the pantry in the dark of night to pilfer the butter

- How he would enthusiastically deliver a huge and forceful wave at almost every person he drove past, calling each unknown and unmet friend 'John-Joe' and every woman 'Mary.'

- How he would stick his tongue out of the side of his mouth when he concentrated

- How he would so carefully select his shirt, tie, and cardigan each day and wear them with pizazz and flair

- When he walked into a room, you knew he was there

- He was full of the childish mischief of a young boy

- He loved living near the sea

- That he was truly loved by so many

- His love of rum and raisin ice cream

- How when he ate something he really loved, he wouldn't speak and his eyes would roll up in his head from sheer pleasure

- That he built a family he loved dearly after losing his own parents while still young

- He helped more people than I will ever know out of their difficulty

- Despite being a large man, women were putty in his hands, but...

- He only had eyes for Mum

- He shared more lessons in life with us than the Bible

- That I have inherited many of his traits and characteristics

These are just some examples of the phenomenal, powerful, personal things I love about HGLD. I could go on and on. And, boy, but I can feel the dopamine, oxytocin, serotonin, and endorphins all doing a bang-up job of supporting me every time I choose to focus on what I love.

Focus on what you love about your special someone, what made them so special to you, and what made you feel special to them. Putting what you love into words then allowing those words and thoughts to take up time and space in your daily routine is powerful, soothing, and stabilizing. This will remind you that the *Love Remains* and that it can and will become your strength as you move forward day by day.

"Keep love in your heart.

A life without it is like a sunless garden when the flowers are dead."

OSCAR WILDE

BABY STEPS

Love is probably the single most transformational, healing, uplifting, and essential component in life. It has the power to change how we feel both physically and emotionally. However, much like a battery, it needs to be topped up or recharged sometimes to supply the much-needed boost of dopamine, oxytocin, serotonin, and endorphins which fuel your positivity, energy, and outlook on life. If you need a helping hand to give yourself a lift or boost your mood, you will find yourself on the right track if you take a little time to recount the things you love about your loved one.

You can make this an all-encompassing, brimming-over, happy-memory-inducing list of *lovely* things that made your loved one so special to you, or perhaps you might switch it up at times to focus on specific topics or aspects of life that are meaningful to you. For instance, you might choose to focus on the things you loved about them in relation to family, friends, special occasions, homelife, daily routines, their humor, food, hobbies, habits, or vacations.

Whichever way you choose to let love in, to remember and focus on the love that remains, you will certainly feel great comfort and spark joy from reliving your memories with your loved one.

You can create your own personal list, you can dip into and borrow from the list of things I love about HGLD above, or you can underline or circle the things below that are most significant to you.

The key to really boosting your emotional well-being is to do this regularly and frequently. Make it part of your daily routine by choosing a time of day, such as first thing in the morning or after dinner when you are ready to relax for the evening, and spend a couple of minutes just focusing on that shared love.

Do it like a word search and connect each 'finding' with a matching memory.

Their unbreakable spirit	Their laugh	The crinkles in their eyes and cheeks when they would laugh
Their resilience	How they would make others feel better about themselves	What a wonderful friend they were to others
How they would go out of their way to help others	Their gentleness	How they knew just what to say to comfort me
Dependability	How they created a home	The stories they would share
Their kindness	Their honesty and integrity	How they would hug me and make me feel safe
How they would make my favorite food	How they got joy from life	When they would blush at and play down compliments
Their willingness to help	How they rocked a colorful scarf/cardigan/shirt/lipstick etc.	How green/blue/brown/purple really brought out their eyes
How we didn't have to speak to understand each other	The joy they got from fresh coffee/ice cream/seafood etc.	Their seriousness when it came to ....
How they would call or show up just when I needed them	How they would put others at ease around them	How they would make sure I was informed of the important stuff
How they loved and cared for me	How they would make me laugh	How they accepted me for who and what I am, exactly as I am
When they would sing out loud	How they encouraged me to be brave	How they believed that everything is possible
Their intelligence and wisdom	How they put their whole heart and soul into what they did	How they snored
The books they read	Their generosity of spirit	Their voice which sounded so ....
Their spontaneity and spirit to try anything once	How they cooked	Their perfume

Freestyle it and make it heartwarmingly personal:

This exercise might feel quite emotional the first time or the first few times you do it. However, by making it a regular feature in your healing process, you will soon begin to find that thinking about your loved one and all the things you love about them provides you with greater comfort, happy memories, and the strength and resilience to tackle the day ahead.

CHAPTER 7:

WHAT I LEARNED FROM HGLD

IF

RUDYARD KIPLING

If you can keep your head when all about you
Are losing theirs and blaming it on you;
If you can trust yourself when all men doubt you,
But make allowance for their doubting too;
If you can wait and not be tired by waiting,
Or, being lied about, don't deal in lies,
Or, being hated, don't give way to hating,
And yet don't look too good, nor talk too wise;

If you can dream, and not make dreams your master;
If you can think, and not make thoughts your aim;
If you can meet with Triumph and Disaster
And treat those two imposters just the same;
If you can bear to hear the truth you've spoken
Twisted by knaves to make a trap for fools,
Or watch the things you gave your life to, broken,
And stoop and build 'em up with worn-out tools;

If you can make one heap of all your winnings
And risk it on one turn of pitch-and-toss,
And lose, and start again at your beginnings
And never breathe a word about your loss;
If you can force your heart and nerve and sinew
To serve your turn long after they are gone,
And so hold on when there is nothing in you
Except the Will which says to them: "Hold on!"

If you can talk with crowds and keep your virtue,
Or walk with kings, nor lose the common touch,
If neither foes nor loving friends can hurt you,
If all men count with you, but none too much;
If you can fill the unforgiving minute
With sixty seconds' worth of distance run,
Yours is the Earth and everything that's in it,
And, which is more, you'll be a Man, my son!

U nlike the majority of other mammals who are born with staggering abilities to fend for themselves (for example, an elephant calf will be capable of standing within minutes and walking within one or two hours after birth), we humans are, by comparision, born considerably less developed and highly dependent on others for survival and growth. In fact, around a whopping 70 percent of our brain is developed after birth. The young depend on the old until gradually the tables are reversed when the old begin to depend on the young. The magical *cycle of life*.

It's through this dependency on others for our very survival that we humans developed our unique sociability and community-forming instincts. From birth, we immediately and innately become pupils, sponges soaking up the information, knowledge, signals, responses, and emotions all around us. This instinct to learn, grow, and develop remains deeply ingrained in us right up to our last breath.

Our relationships and experiences are, to a great extent, the emotional and developmental nourishment through which we grow into the people we become. The most influential relationships, whether with our parents, siblings, teachers, religious leaders, friends, or colleagues, not only provide us with love, support, inspiration, and understanding, but with our most treasured life lessons.

Some of these lessons teach us what *TO do,* and others teach us what *NOT to do.* But they are all the finely balanced ingredients in the recipe of life.

This brings us sliding nicely into the prickly arms of that age-old motto — *No Regrets.* Having no regrets may be the expected party line, but I don't believe in this superficially positive ideology. Certainly, in the case of grieving the loss of someone you love dearly, it might even be a tad unattainable.

How is it even possible to have no regrets? Hand on heart, I have unequivocally learned a great deal from the emotional bruises I have earned along my raggedy, bumpy, less than graceful skid across the oil slick of both life and grief. From time to time, what we learn is the result of something we regret. Horizontal stripes don't do much for rounded hips. My devotion to carbs and, in particular, the humble potato has been misplaced and misguided. Spending years in a relationship that's unhealthy never ends up as time well spent. Forgetting I am driving in the United States versus the United Kingdom and turning left into several lanes of oncoming traffic in Las Vegas isn't good for the heart. Yes, I have some regrets. I learned much from them. I have grown and evolved from them. I am stronger because of them.

One thought that fights for attention in my mind every now and then is wondering what I could and should have done differently for HGLD, particularly toward his final days, weeks, and months. I regret that I couldn't ease his pain. I regret that I didn't get him moved out of the hospital and into the nursing home sooner. I regret that I couldn't spend more time with him in the years before dementia stole him from us as I lived in England and he was in Ireland.

Much like me, Gina has shared with me that when she looks in the rearview mirror of her recent life, she wonders about a great many things that could have been done differently. She wonders if we could have done anything to have made Dad's passing easier for him. Could earlier medical intervention have changed everything and brought him home to us? Could she have said or done anything differently to have comforted or reassured him? She wishes that when he asked her in desperation and extreme and prolonged pain how much longer before this would all be over, she had simply been truthful and said, "Soon," instead of telling him the doctors and nurses would make him better. She regrets not recording him when he told us the stories he loved to indulge in. She wishes we had more time to just be with him in the final two days as he reposed at home before his funeral. She wishes that we had been able to honor him with a more befitting funeral, with everyone there to see him off instead of the tiny congregation of 25 that was allowed to attend.

Sure, it would be fantastic to be able to say you have *no regrets*. But, at least when considering the past, it probably wouldn't be true. The important thing is to learn from it and give yourself permission to move on, with that new knowledge enhancing your future decisions. You can't turn back the clock. You can't go back and change anything in the past. None of us can. So to beat yourself up for your regrets would be futile. Realistically, the 'no regrets' approach to life is only relevant to the present and the future.

The most practical way of having no regrets is if you use that ethos as guidance for how you live your life *today*, here and now, in the present. Using 'no regrets' as a springboard for making better, more fully thought-out, and wiser decisions considering all perspectives. This approach entails sometimes being aware of the necessity of and willingness to do what we *need* to do, not only what we *want* to do.

Having no regrets is also a smart way to plan for the future. We at least have some say in our future decisions. We can bake it into every choice, commitment, and resolution we make going forward, incorporating what we have learned. We can make an agreement with ourselves to accept and embrace our choices. To learn from them, live with them, and to develop as a result of them. That will, at the very least, dramatically reduce our disappointments and regrets. Are you up for that?

The upshot is that it's mighty difficult to live life with no regrets. That would require being able to see into the future so we could make the choices that will give us the outcome we will be happy with. So, until we have mastered time travel, the best we can do is to squeeze every learning we can from the things we regret or wish we had done differently. After all, with hindsight comes great clarity and knowledge.

"I made decisions that I regret and I took them as learning experiences... I'm human, not perfect, like anybody else."

QUEEN LATIFAH

Of course, not all of our life lessons come from regrets or difficult experiences. Some are doled out over the passage of time, gleaned from the character, stories, experiences, guidance, and moments each of us has shared with our own *HGLDs*.

Take a moment now, close your eyes, see *your* 'HGLD.. Bring to mind even just one or two of the wonderful things you learned from them. These could be practical learnings, perhaps how to check the oil level or change a tire on your car, their secret recipe for the perfect sponge cake, how best to manage a difficult conversation with your manager, or how to plant and grow your own herbs or vegetables. They could also be self-esteem building learnings, for example they may have told you how amazing you look when you wear bright colors or helped you to know that you have much to share which can benefit others. Or your golden nuggets of learnings could be of a deeply philosophical nature, daring you to be brave and diverse in your thinking and beliefs. Take a moment and revel in those learnings; let them take up some space and receive them with tenderness and a smile.

From her fiancé Matt, who so sadly passed before they could even marry, Esther learned how hard it can be for someone growing up with health problems, as he had spina bifida. She learned that unfortunately some dads, including Matt's, can be as she would so perfectly put it "rubbish." She learned that if you really want to kick hard drugs you can — this had been one of Matt's demons but one he, with her help, had crushed. Through all these tribulations, Esther learned that *humor* is really important.

Pat carries in her heart the lessons she learned throughout her life from her sister Joy. At the top of her list of lessons was forgiveness and to sometimes just let things be. If something was out of Joy's control, she would let it go and not harbor any ill feelings. After what had been a successful four-year battle against cancer, Joy was given just three months to live and was recommended by her doctors to spend those final precious months in hospice care. Confronting the sobering news, Joy shared with Pat that she was at peace saying, "I have no *pilikia*[1] with anyone." Through Joy, Pat learned to embrace life and live more fully, nurturing relationships. Pat learned to find 'Joy' in the journey. Her sister showed her how to live with no regrets.

Charlene had found that many of her clients learned to live their own lives in a better way because of what they learned from or through the special person they were grieving. In particular, one client recounted how he learned to love from his wife. When thinking about her own father, Charlene explains how he set the bar high for the kind of love that she in turn looked for in her life. She learned she could survive immense loss and even convert it into a meaningful career. She learned how to be kind from her mother and the importance of listening. Her brother taught Charlene to go for her dreams, to not give up, and to believe she could do anything if she put her positive energy into it. She learned how to cook from her grandmother and the healing gifts of her maternal lineage.

Being as close as I am to my sister, growing up together, falling over

---

[1] *Pilikia* is Hawaiian for trouble, animosity, or distress.

and picking each other and ourselves up, we learned many of the same lessons. I can easily see what Dad imparted to her through his actions and words, and how he has influenced who she is as a wife, mother, daughter, sister, and friend. From her precious Pappy, Gina learned and embraced love of family, the importance of building a financial nest egg, the truly connecting value of Christmas, and that hard work, determination, and commitment pay dividends. She learned a deep appreciation for food (*this one may have pros and cons*), how to confidently interact with people on all levels, and the importance of enjoying a hearty laugh and fostering a sense of fun. He bestowed a love for music of all kinds and the uplifting habit of singing to embrace and spread happiness. She learned that the early morning is definitely the best and most productive part of the day. One or two of his lessons, however, are still a work in progress for her (he was a stickler for being on time and an early riser in the morning), but that's okay too.

In addition to what she learned *from* Dad, going through her own personal voyage of grief and loss, Gina has learned that we are all stronger *and* more vulnerable than we realized. She recognizes that we overcome adversity by identifying and using our strengths to support each other and ourselves. She recalls how, in the nursing home, one of the most important things we were told by a lovely nurse was that if we are alone, we are weak, but together we are strong and can get through anything. That particular conversation outside the door of our father's room, just a mere few days before he passed, will never leave either Gina or me. She has learned patience. This patience was lovingly, easily, and willingly embraced while happily waiting in a car park for hours just to get a little look at Dad and receive a smile, wave, or wink from him. She has figured out that her way isn't always the right way. Sometimes it is. But, sometimes there can be three right ways. We can attest to that being more possible and even probable when you put three strong-willed, passionate women like Mum, Gina, and me, together in an emotionally heightened situation!

Gina has found that talking about things and being open to change has fortified her resolve and offered great comfort. Ultimately, Gina has learned that she is stronger than she could have ever imagined and that this strength is a reflection of her support system.

Mum took a wealth of learnings from her decades-long relationship with Dad. Firstly, she recalls how through his support of and faith in her, she learned to become independent from the very day they married. That independence is something she carries with her now as she learns to cope with her loss and a whole new way of life on her own. When Mum succeeds at simple yet deceptively difficult things, such as staying alone at night, she thanks Dad for the independence he proudly cultivated in her. Without his belief in her, she would never have thought she could do it. She learned to enjoy the simple things in life, like spending quality time together and watching the birds visit their beautiful garden for a never-ending supply of every kind of bird food. Mum, a novice in the kitchen, remembers how she burned the first dinner she ever cooked for Dad after they married to an unrecognizable charred crisp. His much-anticipated dinner resembled a long-forgotten sausage that had escaped a last-minute dash for liberation through the wire rack of the raging barbeque, or perhaps even the fires of hell. It went right into the bin and so began the cookery lessons. Dad, a great cook and prolific lover of food, was happy to teach his trainee chef. As Mum explains it, he couldn't live on love alone.

I doubt that I have lived a single day without pondering or putting into practice one of the juicy, rich assortment of HGLD's *braindrops* as I like to call all those juicy life lessons he shared with me through his love, experience, knowledge, and huge appetite for life.

We all have lessons that we have gleaned from our loved ones. Some may have been tough lessons that molded or protected us, while others were perhaps gentle lessons that allowed us space to think, adapt, and grow. You also may have benefitted from the wisdom and guidance of your loved one. Take a quiet moment, close your eyes, and think about the wisdom they imparted to you and how it has not only helped you in specific situations but remained with you and become part of what now makes you... you.

Here are some of Dad's assorted lessons or *braindrops* that have guided me well. You might have a similar list of colorful learnings from your *'HGLD'* which have guided you and helped form who you are today. There is a *Baby Steps* exercise coming up to help you capture what you have embraced from them and how these special insights are going to continue to enhance your life.

HGLD's Braindrops

- *If you don't ask, you don't get.* This was never, ever intended from a greedy, 'I want more' perspective but from bravery. Dad taught me to stand up and be counted. To always be the first to put my hand up, whether to ask a question, to offer help, or say yes to an opportunity.

- *If you love what you're doing, you'll never work a day in your life.* I'm sure I've heard this one more times than I've had hot dinners. But it's so true. We may not all be in our ideal job at any given time, but this braindrop was about taking accountability for our choices. It was about finding joy in what we do. It was also about being willing to put in the effort to get from where you are to where you want to be. That's the real differentiator.

- *If a thing's worth doing, it's worth doing well.* He had neither the time nor the tolerance for shortcuts, being wise enough and long enough in the tooth to know that shortcuts ultimately take longer and generally result in redoing the work, more effort, and frustration. He was a man who took pride in doing something well, and let's just say that the apple didn't fall far from the tree.

- *Up there (touching the head) for thinking, down there (pointing to feet) for dancing.* By this he meant quite simply to engage your brain rather than just step into something without thinking. This would be frequently alternated with...

- *Think it through then follow it through.* His version of 'measure twice and cut once.' Dad was big on thinking, on truly looking at a situation, and only then taking action. Not to say that he was a ditherer — far from it. His mind, up until dementia took hold of him in the final few years, was a finely tuned precision machine. But thinking, weighing up the facts and angles, and planning were all as critical to him as the action to follow.

- *Bing, bing, bing.* This was used to great effect to ensure that following through after the thinking through of any situation was seen as simple, straightforward, and second nature, and would go something like this, "Once you have figured out what it is that you need to do, just identify the very first step, then bing, bing, bing!" The implication being that the momentum will carry you if you have planned well.

- *Never borrow tractors.* As intriguing as this one sounds, and it is, I'm going to ask your indulgence to bear with me for now, otherwise it will require a spoiler alert for the final chapter of this book. Now I've got you wondering but it's a great little story and worth the wait.

- *Break their arm off.* This was the encouragement that inevitably and immediately accompanied an amped-up twinkle in his eye when we would discuss any opportunity that crossed my path which would result in my development. HGLD was totally on board with regretting doing something rather than regretting not taking the chance. What do you have to lose? Do it. You will figure it out.

- *Never go to sleep on an argument.* Search for the agreement. Pick your battles wisely. Agree to disagree. This was pretty much all the relationship advice Dad would proffer and, as far as he was concerned, it applied to all relationships. I have to admit I fully agree and have found that, while in practice it might not always be easy, palatable, or even possible, it certainly is the aspiration.

These and more of HGLD's *braindrops* can be found in the Glossary at the end of *Love Remains* for you to dip into any time you feel like a little inspirational tip.

There is a virtual and veritable smorgasbord of *braindrops* to inspire me to make great life choices, take action, and share with others in their time of quandary or need. These beautiful memories have become the life lessons that give me courage, direction, and peace of mind. Best of all, they are filed away in my head and heart and ready to help and cheer me at a moment's notice.

I know you too have a cornucopia of *braindrops* that have been lovingly and thoughtfully shared with you and stored away in your mind, ready to help you navigate life's decisions and tricky situations.

One of the greatest gifts you get to enjoy from the relationships you build throughout your life is the abundance of inspiring, transformational, and empowering learnings these relationships offer. Some are shared purposefully and directly in order to help you through difficult moments or decisions. Others you learn by watching, listening, and being open to the innate wisdom of someone you love, respect, and hold in high esteem. Best of all, these nuggets of wisdom remain with you forever, like a silent yet familiar inner voice helping you to navigate difficult situations, to make stronger and more informed decisions, and perhaps to feel comfort and strength of conviction.

When you find you need a little inspiration or something to nudge you gently onward, add *one large spoon of the wisdom of great minds*. Great minds are all around you, dipping in and out of your everyday life in the form of your family, friends, colleagues, people you share a smile with as you walk past, and, most assuredly, your special loved one.

You too will undoubtedly have a wonderful list of lessons about love and life from your *'HGLD.'* Embrace their *braindrops*, welcome them in, and take time to remember and bask in those little nuggets of wisdom. In doing this, you will create space in your heart, mind, and life for these special sharings to remain with you; healing, supporting, empowering, and comforting you forever.

> *"I learned most, not from those who taught me,*
> *but from those who talked with me."*
>
> SAINT AUGUSTINE

BABY STEPS

Braindrops **from my loved one**

Every important relationship in our lives gives us so much more than love, security, friendship, companionship, and encouragement. They also give us pearls of wisdom, guidance, and perspective which truly have the power to enhance our lives, particularly as they come from people we trust and value.

We are constantly learning, growing, and evolving, whether we stop to realize it or not. We soak up all the overt and sometimes more covert lessons our loved ones cared enough to share in our time together.

Take your time, pour yourself a cup of tea or coffee, sit in your favorite chair, and allow all the braindrops *your 'HGLD'* shared with you to flood back into your mind and onto the page.

Recounting these lessons is a great way to keep them with us in heart, mind, and action. It's also an excellent opportunity to honor their willingness to help and to inspire us by finding ways we can share those *braindrops* onward to others. That's their true and powerful legacy.

What I learned	How it has shaped me	How I can share it onward
Example: I am enough already, exactly as I am.	Encouraged my self-worth and self-confidence.	Talk kindly to others and encourage them to be less self-critical. Lead by example.
I can achieve anything I set my mind to.	Gave me the confidence to say yes to opportunities and adventures throughout my life.	Remind my daughter and my niece that they can do anything, achieve anything if they choose, plan, and work for it.

Transforming Regrets into Lifelong Learnings

Some of our greatest life lessons are the result of things that didn't quite work out exactly as we'd hoped or planned. It's through those experiences that we have the valuable opportunity to consider what we would do differently if we had that chance for a 'do-over' or how we might tackle a similar situation in the future.

Even thinking about what made our loved ones who have passed so special to us and all the things we miss about them can raise regrets. We might wish that we had listened to them more, spent more time with them, not put off plans, or told them we loved them more often.

The danger of not finding and mentally registering the learning from our past experiences is the potential to repeat our mistakes in the future. In overlooking the learning, we risk living with guilt and regret. Particularly when the things we wished we did differently are in relation to our loved one who has passed, the guilt of regret can be a heavy burden to carry. It's a burden your loved one would not wish for you to bear and it's one that you can give yourself permission to set down and to move past to feel wiser and more at peace with yourself.

This exercise offers you a simple technique to find your learnings, to accept and let go of the past regrets, and to focus on how you will move forward, better prepared and more confident about the future.

What I regret	Why I regret it	What I will do differently in the future
Examples: Not making time to visit HGLD more often in his final year or two.	I assumed that he would still have time but his time was running out. I allowed the long journey and my busy life to be the reasons I visited him less frequently.	Make the time to spend time with those I love. Never assume that there will be more time.
Not having him moved from the hospital and into the nursing home sooner.	He might have had a chance to recover.	Listen to my intuition and intervene or challenge what I believe is wrong. In the case of someone's welfare, don't hesitate to react when my intuition tells me to.
Not writing down HGLD's stories.	I can't recall all the details and won't have all his stories to share with my grandchildren when they come along.	Capture what I can recall and save it to share with and inspire my grandchildren in years to come.

You may find that you need to come back to this exercise more than once to work through any regrets or missed opportunities that surface as you focus on and give head and heart space to the things you love and miss about your *'HGLD'* through the *Baby Steps* in *Love Remains* or as they swirl around you and bubble up in your day-to-day life, thoughts, and memories.

Through this resilience-building exercise, you will give yourself permission to be human and to forgive your mistakes. You will also empower yourself to make positive changes in your life going forward. Now that you know what changes to make, think about how you can start putting some of those learnings into practice.

CHAPTER 8:

WHAT I AM GRATEFUL TO HGLD FOR

THAT MAN IS A SUCCESS

ROBERT LOUIS STEVENSON

That man is a success
who has lived well,
laughed often and loved much;
who has gained the respect of intelligent men and women
and the love of children;
who has filled his niche and accomplished his task;
who leaves the world better than he found it,
Who never lacked appreciation of earth's beauty
or failed to express it;
who looked for the best in others,
and gave the best he had.

Have you noticed how gratitude has become something of a super buzzword in recent years? You could sink, or perhaps it's more appropriate to say float, an ocean liner with the articles, advice, meditations, and so much more extolling the many virtues of this noun which, when treated as a verb, has near magical powers of transformation.

Gratitude can come in the form of a few kind words that we either give or receive from others. These simple exchanges ignite something special, with its own momentum, and the power to transform and lift us. And, when gratitude becomes a habit, we strengthen the neural pathways which lead to greater, more frequent, and readily available happiness, contentment, and positive nature.

In daily life we must see that it is not happiness that makes us grateful, but gratefulness that makes us happy.

BENEDICTINE MONK, AUTHOR, AND LECTURER, DAVID STEINDL-RAST

Many studies have been made into the effects of gratitude on our physical and mental health. I'm sure you won't be even remotely surprised that all signs point to the betterment of our well-being when you incorporate gratitude into your life. Research from the Mindfulness Awareness Research Center of UCLA found that gratitude changes the neural structures in the brain and makes us feel happier and more content. A study by The Journal of Positive Psychology found that gratitude exceeded forgiveness, patience, and self-control in predicting hope and happiness. The same study found that writing about one's gratitude can bolster present happiness and hope for the future.

In fact, the effects of the regular practice of gratitude, for example establishing a daily habit of recalling or writing down three things you were grateful for in the day as it is coming to a close or keeping a daily gratitude journal, are widely accepted to be a natural and freely available antidepressant due to how gratitude is irrefutably linked to the release of many feel-good neurochemicals and hormones such as our good ol' friends serotonin, dopamine, and oxytocin. All the internal goodies that are associated with mood regulation, well-being, healthy sleep patterns, happiness, and even pain management. The regular practice of gratitude has also been shown to reduce the stress hormones cortisol and adrenaline. What's not to like?

A healthy dose of gratitude can also result in reducing inflammation, stimulating anti-inflammatory responses in the body, and for some people, even reversing the autoimmune process. Studies have linked a daily gratitude practice with the reduction of an inflammatory marker in the body which is often elevated in patients with autoimmune conditions.

Due in part to how our bodies and minds are positively impacted by these feel-good natural chemicals, we are as a direct result more willing and likely to engage in activities that further support us, such as exercise, social interaction, work, projects, and, on a more critical and basic level, self-care. This sparks a powerful, positive cycle of *action* leading to the release of *neurotransmitters*, the body's chemical messengers, resulting in *positive feelings*, which fuel more *action*... and so it continues.

All these incredible biochemical benefits stimulate our physical and mental well-being and, amazingly, can be obtained from a simple, regular practice which is completely within our control.

We are highly unlikely to ever be grateful for the loss of someone special, other than perhaps because their pain and suffering has ended. However the very fact that we are grieving the loss of them from our lives is testimony to how much we have to be grateful for as a result of that relationship. If there was nothing to be grateful for, there's no significant role for grief when they go.

Your ability to look through and beyond the pain of your loss and to focus intentionally on what you are grateful for about that relationship honors the time, connection, and love you shared. You will find, over time, that regularly bringing to mind those beautiful memories, moments, experiences, and emotions that connected you together then concluding each memory consciously with something along the lines of: "I'm grateful for the opportunity we had to _____," becomes a practice you enjoy and gain strength from.

When Esther looks back on her relationship with Matt, she feels lucky that she met someone who was right for her, that they shared 12 years of each other's lives, and that she was able to give him the support he needed which gave him a happy life. They had some amazing experiences together, such as traveling around Australia and Europe. Esther is grateful that Matt wanted them to get a gorgeous chocolate labrador dog called Archie, who meant the world to her until he passed away at a ripe old age, leaving countless loving memories behind with him. She has a lovely relationship with Matt's sister and family, and even his Dad and Stepmum from whom Matt was estranged. They have been a terrific support for both Esther and, in more recent years, her little boy JJ.

Pat loves that she was often mistaken as Joy's twin, a little inside joke both ladies enjoyed. Pat feels that, in reality, they were spiritual twins where Joy was the leader and Pat the Chief of Staff, making sure things got done. Joy was her hero and Pat was shocked to learn that she was, in turn, Joy's hero. Right up until the very end, Joy was Pat's biggest cheerleader and the reason she dared to return to performing onstage and camera again. Pat can still hear her words, "Follow your destiny," and will always be grateful that Joy continues to be the wind beneath her wings.

Throughout her years of helping others deal with their grief, Charlene has found that most of her clients have a deep gratitude for the relationship they had with the person they are grieving and for seeing the ways that connection continues on in their memories and how they live their lives. On a personal level, Charlene is grateful for every one of the loved ones she has lost for she cherishes the lessons learned and the love they shared.

Mum is exceptionally grateful for the 56 years she shared with Dad, 54 of them in a highly successful and supportive marriage. These, to both Mum and Dad, were immensely happy, fulfilling years. So much so that she would marry him all over again without even a moment's hesitation. She is forever grateful to Dad for my sister and me and for the brilliant father he was to us.

Gina, being a kind and loving soul who has had and still lives with her own lengthy catalog of daily debilitating medical issues, is adept at finding and embracing her gratitude. When thinking about her Pappy, she is always grateful for knowing and feeling loved by him. For his colorful storytelling every night when we were little girls. For all the fun times we had as children when he would make an indoor camp involving all kinds of paraphernalia. How he would make us a tea party of Angel Delight (a raspberry-flavored mousse dessert), Hula Hoops (little packets of crisps shaped like rings which we would jam onto our tiny fingers and eat from there), and orange squash served in a red plastic doll's tea set. How he would help us to tie long elastics together to make a French Skipping (Double Dutch) rope from which we would get hours of enjoyment and exercise. All the Sunday afternoon drives, singing songs along the way. Trips into and around the factory he worked in. And his understanding, at least most of the time, when she was in trouble and had been sent to her room. That he always would find time to spend with us as little girls in the evening regardless of how late or tired he arrived home from work. He always had time to talk to us. She will always be grateful for having him in her life for 53 years. *One liberal sprinkling of gratitude* buoys her up in times of need.

He was human and fallible, like we all are, but as I think about how immeasurably lucky I was to have had HGLD in my life and how I continue to evolve and benefit from his input, example, parables, character, and presence, I know as sure as the sun will rise tomorrow that I have no shortage of things to be grateful for.

In just the same way, even while grieving for your *'HGLD,'* you can welcome into your words, heart, and life the state of mind and immune-boosting benefits of gratitude just by taking a few moments to recount what made them so special to you.

Finding what you are grateful for begins with recognizing or recalling the things you enjoyed or benefitted from as a result of the good intentions or positive actions of someone else. You can start by focusing on your loved one and what it was about them or what effect and impact they had and still have on your life that you are grateful for. Then you can broaden the scope and focus on what you are grateful for by considering your life today and those who do their best to make it a little better. For example, you may have some wonderful friends and family members who each provide love, connection, support, a listening ear, and company, all in their own unique ways. You might then look beyond your close circle of supporters to the organizations that have played a positive role in your life, whether that's a book club, a support group, a class you participate in, or it might even be people you pass by on the street who, without knowing you, share a smile or hold a door open for you to pass first.

As I share some things I am grateful for, keep *your 'HGLD'* in mind and make room for a little lightness and love in your heart. There is a *Baby Steps* exercise coming up to help you capture what you are grateful for regarding the person you loved.

Things I'm Grateful to HGLD for

- The creative magic he would sprinkle, when he could, into our childhood through mythical, mystical, and often madcap stories and adventures that would enthrall us, where anything could happen. There were no rules; his imagination would run riot, whipping us up with it along the way.

- How he would come straight to our bedrooms to tuck us in at night when he returned from work, usually with a sweet treat hidden in his pocket.

- That he loved spending time with us and was entirely good with us snuggling up to his large and comforting frame as he would watch TV from his favorite armchair.

- The amazing roast dinner he would enjoy cooking every Sunday with plenty of succulent tender but well-done beef and no shortage of beautifully crisped roast potatoes and lashings of gravy. Hmmmmmm.

- The extravaganza of blockbuster proportions when he made the roast turkey dinner every Christmas and how he would pull out all the stops to ensure we all had what we wanted, and lashings of it.

- How he made Christmas so special for us all. Some years he dressed up as Santa Claus to hand out gifts to the children at the factory Christmas party. Every Christmas morning he would lock the living room door where the tree and presents were (not fair!) while he got the meal of epic proportions underway so he could be ready with his prized old-style — though brand new back then in the 1970s — cine camera in hand to capture every squeal of delight as his two little princesses flittered open their gifts.

- The love, adoration, and security he devoted to Mum. Caring for her was undoubtedly his purpose for breathing.

- That he was a tireless mentor to anyone who showed signs of promise, passion, or potential. In my case, I knew that he would never, ever say no if I came to him for advice or to just mull something over. He was giving of his time, knowledge, and his ear.

- That he had faith in me and what I was capable of, even when I didn't.

- His sense of humor which provided great balance to all the times of pressure.

- His infectious 'can-do' attitude. No mountain was ever too high, no problem too great, no situation impossible.

- The memories I get to keep forever of all our times together, lessons shared, love nurtured. Forever mine to hold, glean comfort from, use, reuse, develop further, and share onward with others.

All these memories, the character traits, habits, and special gifts, of the one *you* love dearly are the legacy they leave behind, etched indelibly into your life. These are the things you are grateful for, that continue to light up your face when you think of them with a smile that spreads with sincerity from your cheeks to your eyes. These are the memories that warm your heart, inspire your life, and make carrying on day-by-day that little bit lighter, easier, and better just by recognizing with gratitude their impact and the impact of others on your life. Yes, so much remains. So many blessings to count. So much gratitude to fill your heart with love and thankfulness for all that you have enjoyed.

> *"When I started counting my blessings,*
> *my whole life turned around".*
> WILLIE NELSON

BABY STEPS

Allow yourself the gift of some much-needed and well-deserved serotonin, dopamine, and oxytocin, all those feel-good neurotransmitters and hormones which will uplift, strengthen, and happify you, even while grieving.

Clear your mind of all other tasks and diversions and focus on *your* 'HGLD,' the relationship you had, the experiences you shared, how you have grown just by being in their life. For each happy memory that comes to mind, focus on how it makes you grateful.

1. What I Am Grateful for Thanks to _____

In this case, practice really does make perfect. The more you consciously and purposefully practice gratitude, the easier and more natural it becomes. The more you find, think, and talk about what you are grateful for, the sooner it makes it easier to talk about your loved one, which in turn lifts your mood, aids sleep, manages pain, makes things eminently more copeable, and opens you up to what lies ahead with renewed confidence and peace.

What I am grateful for	How it has shaped me	How I can share it onward
Example: How he taught me to be brave and worthy	Gave me the foundation and belief to make brave choices, to learn from them, and to see them through	Encourage my daughter to make brave choices and to hold herself accountable

2. Going to Bed with Gratitude and Waking Up with Love

You will feel the greatest emotional and physical benefits of gratitude when you widen out the practice and apply it, not only considering your loved one, but your daily life. Even while grieving for your loved one who has passed, if you really look for it, gratitude is there to be found in the kindness, love, and support of those around you.

Bedtime Gratitude:

Here's what to do:

1. When you are in bed and ready to welcome sleep, recall three things you were grateful for during that day. These can be small and seemingly inconsequential, such as noticing a flower in your garden or that someone smiled at you. Or, they can be big and impactful, such as a major win at work or a friend or family member who you know is looking out for you.

2. If you get stuck occasionally in finding three *new* things from that day, have a few standby things you are grateful for to fall back on. For example, these could be something specific about your body, sight, hearing, flexibility, strength, job, hobbies, favorite restaurant or garden, flowers you bought yourself, the daily newspaper, or a regular podcast or exercise class to name just a few.

Example: I'm grateful for the opportunity I had for a coffee and chat today with my sister who always has my back.
1
2
3

By doing this right before sleeping, you will end your day on a more positive note and, particularly when practiced regularly, this can reduce the production of the stress hormones cortisol and adrenaline. You can additionally benefit from a boost of the feel-good neurotransmitters and hormones which support healthy sleep patterns and general well-being. Build this into your nightly routine and you will soon begin to feel these positive shifts both physically and emotionally.

Waking up with love:

This exercise is similar to 'Bedtime Gratitude' in that it calls for you to bring to mind the positive aspects in your life, but this time the focus is a little different; the focus is on *YOU*. Particularly what you like, love, or appreciate about yourself. This might feel strange and a bit self-serving but it is important to begin to treat and talk to yourself with love, appreciation, and kindness. I'm sure you find it easy to say nice, kind, caring, and morale-boosting yet truthful things to the people you love and care about. That ability to see the good in others should be a 'two-way street' and will become more authentic in its intention and effect when you treat and talk to yourself with the same kindness.

Here's what to do:

1. When you are waking up and getting ready to face the new day, bring to mind three things you like or love about yourself. These can be apparently inconsequential, such as loving how the color purple makes your eyes pop or that you bake incredible cupcakes. Alternatively, they can be the big game changers like being a brilliant mother/father/sibling/daughter/son or that you make a difference to others through your work or friendships.

2. If you get stuck occasionally in finding three *new* things to like or love about yourself, either have a few standby things to fall back on or think from the perspective of your loved one and give yourself permission to appreciate the things they loved about you too. The things you love or like about yourself might,

for instance, include your hair thickness, color, or length, your eyes, your writing, your ability to care for your family or friends, that you go out of your way to help others, how a particular color brightens you up and makes your eyes shine, how patient you are when you explain something new to someone, your cooking, or how you create a wonderful family environment.

Example: I love how I make a difference in other people's lives just by sharing my time with them.
1
2
3

When you make gratitude and self-love a daily practice, you will find it's a great way to regain some balance and recognize that while you miss your loved one dearly, you continue to honor the life that they would want you to live with love, confidence, and strength.

CHAPTER 9:

THE ONE WHERE....

IN LIEU OF FLOWERS

SHAWNA LEMAY

Although I love flowers very much, I won't see them when I'm gone.
So in lieu of flowers:
Buy a book of poetry written by someone still alive,
sit outside with a cup of tea, a glass of wine,
and read it out loud, or silenty,
by yourself or to someone.
Spend some time with a single flower.
A rose maybe.
Smell it, touch the petals.
Really look at it.
Drink a nice bottle of wine with someone you love. Or, Champagne.
And think of what John Maynard Keynes said,
"My only regret in life is that I did not drink more Champagne."
Or what Dom Perignon said when he first tasted the stuff:
"Come quickly! I am tasting stars!"
Take out a paint set and lay down some colours.
Watch birds. Common sparrows are fine.
Pigeons, too. Geese are nice. Robins.
In lieu of flowers, walk in the trees and watch the light fall into it.
Eat an apple, a really nice big one.
I hope it's crisp.

Have a long soak in the bathtub with can-
dles, maybe some rose petals.
Sit on the front stoop and watch the clouds.
Have a dish of strawberry ice cream in my name.
If it's winter, have a cup of hot chocolate outside for me.
If it's summer, a big glass of ice water.
If it's autumn, collect some leaves and press them in a book you love.
I'd like that.
Sit and look out a window and write down what you see.
Write some other things down.
In lieu of flowers,
I would wish for you to flower.
I would wish for you to blossom, to open, to be beautiful.
I wish for you to align your soul, for a time, with flowers.

I am sure that your mind, much like mine, is packed full of the experiences and stories that have filled your life up to now. Some amazing, some good, some not so good, and some you'd much rather forget. It's all in the mix of your one-of-a-kind life's journey. These memories you have stored in the scrapbook of your mind pop up every now and then, particularly when triggered by a place, smell, familiar song, name, color, or an event or situation.

What if, when you need an emotional lift, instead of waiting for the memories to bubble up to the top of your thoughts of their own accord, you could welcome them to sit awhile with you, keep you company, offer companionship, reassurance, inner strength, shared smiles, and a healing virtual hug? All on demand. Yes, you can, even while missing your loved one. I would like to share with you a simple technique to do exactly that and how it gave me and my family a much-needed lift.

During his final months, we rallied to do everything even remotely conceivable to care for Dad, initially with the burning desire to get him better and return him home to the life he loved with the woman he had adored since he first laid eyes on her. Then we, each at our own speed, eventually, grudgingly, and heart-shatteringly acquiesced to the devastating realization that this was not going to happen. We began to focus all our powers, efforts, intentions, thoughts, hearts, and prayers on Dad's comfort. Spending every minute we were allowed around him. Ensuring Mum was free of all other tasks and obligations so she could devote herself entirely to being by his side. Monitoring his needs, calling for medication, sharing quiet time, and chatting with him. Chatting *with* Dad was very much wishful thinking as it was increasingly a case of chatting *to* him as he slipped further away from us and into the depths of dementia. All this as the grains in the sand timer measuring what was left of his life escaped, almost defiantly and in disdain at our futile efforts to hold onto him. Each precious grain of sand, dropped irreversibly grain by grain, every single one falling with a silently thundering, echoing crash which rang like terror in our ears.

Intense sadness, fear, and stress surrounded us like an insulated, impenetrable bubble. But, as we fought the inevitable, we found ourselves dipping in and out of all our comforting, loving, quirky, and fun recountings of Dad. Adding *one or two portions of humor* every now and then was a tonic which gave us the fortitude to carry on, day by day.

It was in this highly fraught and surreal existence, as we honed all our attention and focus on Dad, that my sister, my true soulmate, defender and best friend, had an inspired stroke of genius. We would create *a memory jar.*

Gina's inspired idea was for the three of us, Mum, Gina, and me, to each capture any little funny stories or memories which brought us joy, happiness, smiles, or fuzzy feelings on small sheets of paper taken from a square notepad, fold each one up, and place it in a memory jar. This would give us a ready-made source of uplifting moments, giggles, and connection when we would need it most. I had heard about memory jars before and knew they had provided great comfort and happiness to others but hadn't thought about making one, filled with delightfully touching memories of Dad, until Gina suggested it.

We set about the task immediately and instantly felt our energy shift for the better.

We found a perfect, small, pretty jar that had fulfilled its original destiny as the safekeeper of some of the finest raspberry jam to be found in our county. Gina washed it thoroughly, soaking it in hot water until she could peel off the sticky label, and with some modicum of anticipation and a twinkle in her eye, she set it empty between us on the coffee table.

Next we commandeered the notepad, the kind which often resides next to the house phone, along with a few pens that aided in our task. Then Mum, Gina and I gathered around the coffee table, ready to recall and capture some of our fondest and most uplifting memories to bolster us and to relish in the future.

Memory jar? *Check.*

Writing instruments? *Check.*

Happy memories? *Check. Check. Check.*

As we started writing, never one to be short of a great idea, Gina then came up with a theme that was sure to always connect these magnificent mini memoirs with happiness. If you, like we, are a fan of the utterly brilliant television sitcom *Friends*, you will possibly have noticed that the title of every inspirational episode of the show begins with 'The one where…' We embraced that simple but effective and fun approach and started our personal reminisces with those same words at the top of every little square of paper. We soon found that it became unimportant to provide copious detail in our recounted stories on each square of paper as that colorful detail is tattooed for all time in our hearts and minds. Just the title and the core funny or endearing aspect of the story were often sufficient.

On each blank square of paper we captured a special moment shared with Dad. Every single one made us smile, laugh, share meaningful looks, or shed a few tears, and even sometimes mortify us into rosy blushes of embarrassment.

Once captured, we then folded the note in half and half again, and each inspirational ditty or moving memory was placed with love into the jar.

As the days went by, we continued to add more love and more stories into *'Our Little Jar of Happy Moments'* when the notion would catch us and a rib-tickling or heartstring-plucking tale would come to mind.

Creating a memory jar and adding our personal reminiscences of all the funny, tender, special, joyful, and meaningful things about Dad that made him unique, and our time with him precious, not only provided us with immense comfort, many laughs, and a heartening flood of happy recollections but also with the certainty and security that comes from knowing *he* lives on in our hearts and memories.

You, I am sure, also have amassed many poignant, comforting, and happy stories, experiences, and special moments from your time with *your* 'HGLD.' Those special times that underpin the unique character, gifts, and lifetime of your loved one are yours to keep forever. They will offer you strength, reassurance, and the warm glow of love and happiness as you recount these memories and all the things that made your loved one so important, influential, and special in your life.

Here's a little selection of what we put into our jar. As you read on, I encourage you to think about *your* 'HGLD' and what sweet memories you might want to capture for your own little jar of happy moments.

The one where... I gently squeezed Pappy's hand three times and said, "I love you," and he tapped his hand on the bed three times to say, "I love you," back. That meant the world to me.

The one where... I was chatting in his room with a nurse and Dad opened up his eyes, and when he looked like he was going to speak, we both eagerly listened only to be asked, "Can I sleep please?" in a frank and frustrated tone.

The one where... It was Mammy and Pappy's 54th wedding anniversary and they had a surprise visit from his favorite cousins. Well, Pappy's face when he saw his cousin Mary was a picture of pure delight. I was so lucky to capture it in a photograph. Precious moments.

The one where... Pappy took the unopened little love letter I gave him from Mammy, and very carefully inhaled the smell of her Chanel No. 5™ perfume, which Mammy sprayed on the envelope, and tucked it most carefully inside his pajamas top, near his heart, and held his hand over it to keep it safe.

The one where... Bob was outside cutting the grass on his ride-on mower and he stopped at the kitchen window to wave in at me. This became a little ritual every time he cut the grass. What a beautiful memory.

The one where... While sitting with Dad in the nursing home, my chair pulled right up beside him, he opened up his hand and looked expectantly at me until I put my hand in his. He then folded his other hand around it and tucked our joined hands up under his pillow and fell happily asleep. Pure joy, along with a smattering of cramps and 'pins and needles' due to being in a strangely contorted position for a considerable amount of time, but no way was I going to break this spell.

The one where... While lying in his bed in the nursing home, he took my newspaper from me and tucked it under his arm so I wasn't distracted from him. When I thought he was asleep I tried to sneak it back again for a read but he smiled at me, with eyes still closed, and held on tighter to my paper.

The one where... With his finger he beckoned me to come closer (he had no energy to speak) as he lay in his nursing home bed. When I was close enough, he pointed at my mask, then pulled at it, pinging it back onto my face. He wanted me to remove the mask…. because he wanted a kiss.

The one where… I was excited to spend the day with Pappy in the nursing home so I wore my favorite perfume. It was the one that happily reminded us all of Nana, who Pappy adored. As I leaned over to greet him with a hug, I was informed quite categorically, "I don't like your smell. Go away!" Knowing this was the dementia talking, I went away, laughing, to wash every last remnant of perfume off me!

The one where… Pappy surprised me by drinking two beakers of apple juice, two beakers of orange cordial, and two beakers of 7-Up™ (a fizzy lemon lime drink), a mini tub of dessert mousse, and two squares of Turkish Delight™ chocolate. All this when he had been outright refusing to eat or drink for some time. He really enjoyed the taste of the Turkish Delight but it took me ages to get the chocolate out of his beard!

The one where… He removed one of his medicated skin patches and rolled it up into a ball. When I asked him to give it to me, so I could dispose of it and inform the nurse, he cheekily threw it across the room with every ounce of strength he had, not breaking eye contact with me for even a second! A petulant childlike moment which made me laugh so much.

The one where… My thoughtful partner, knowing how much Dad loved a good burger but also that he had all but stopped eating, arranged for a take-out delivery to the nursing home. I unwrapped the huge, juicy, fully loaded burger and started to eat it right there in front of him. Recent experience had taught me that asking or begging him to eat was futile. The succulent aromas broke through barriers we thought were unbreakable and he started licking his lips as I took a bite. Only then did I dare ask if he would like some. To my immense shock, he took the burger in his hands and proceeded to eat three bites! More than he had eaten in weeks. He was so smack-dab in the middle of a blissful experience that his eyes rolled up in his head. Magic!

The lightness, comfort, and connection the contents of that special little jar gives me is undeniable. Simply knowing that jar is there for me to dip into at will makes the air that little bit fresher and my step a little lighter. Now, any time I feel a wave of sorrow bubble up within me, I can reach into the *Little Jar of Happy Moments* and instantly feel that wave dissolve away to be replaced with happy memories full of love.

You too deserve the comfort, consolation, and joy that can be found from keeping the anecdotes of *your* 'HGLD' in a *Little Jar of Happy Moments*. They are your precious memories to keep, savor, and enjoy alone or with others as you reminisce together about your special someone.

However you decide to bring the happy memories you have of your loved one to mind, they are the twinkling stars that will light you up today, tomorrow, and forever. These loving, funny, sincere, happy memories are *yours to keep*, to replay, to sustain you, to warm the cockles of your heart, and to remind you of all the beautiful memories and 'The Ones where...'

> *"If there ever comes a day when we can't be together,*
>
> *keep me in your heart, I'll stay there forever."*
>
> WINNIE THE POOH

BABY STEPS

Just like in years gone by we used to keep a photo album and haul it out when visitors would come over in order to share the treasures of the past, having a little jar of happy memories at hand may provide you with a much-needed boost when you really need it. Like a photo album, reach for it when you want to relive a few memories. Sit down and enjoy dipping into your jar of wonders with a cup of something warm on a quiet afternoon, or share some memories with your nearest and dearest when they come to visit.

The stories, adventures, experiences, and celebrations you capture can be simple silly stuff like shared jokes, comical mishaps, or misunderstandings that resulted in laughter, or the bigger, deep, and momentous moments like your first date together, your wedding day, or another momentous celebration, like the birth of a child or the adventures of traveling to far-flung exotic places. Find those moments that brought forth your wonder, awe, excitement, fun, or joy, those moments that remind you why your *'HGLD'* was so special and unique to you and to others. Each and every moment is yours to keep and recall over and over, to savor and take immense pleasure in every time you read them.

Creating Your Own Little Jar of Happy Moments

Here's what to do:

1. Find your jar. This can be as simple as a jam jar you were ready to recycle, a shoe box you have covered in pretty wrapping paper, a vase, or a beautiful wooden box.

2. Keep a little block of square notes (not sticky notes) at hand beside the jar and a pen.

3. Start by capturing the first happy memories or funny stories that come to mind.

4. Feel free to borrow our 'The one where...' approach.

5. Don't overthink it. It's not about perfect prose, detail, or getting the grammar right. It's *your* memories and special moments with your loved one. The times you shared that made you laugh, feel happy, secure, and loved, and most particularly the throw-your-head-back-laughing moments. Find the joy and capture each one on a little square, then fold it in half and in half again.

6. Ask others to contribute their stories also.

7. Add more as they pop into your mind. It's amazing how sights, sounds, smells, tastes, and touch will bring you back to those moments.

8. Dip into your jar for some happy memories either on your own or share the experience with those closest to you.

Creating and dipping into your own *Little Jar of Happy Moments* every now and then is incredibly healing and heartening. These are your personal, 100 percent authentic treasures, and will offer you the comfort of a cashmere blanket or perhaps a shot of joy or some light in the tunnel just when you need it the most.

CHAPTER 10:

THE MOST WONDERFUL TIME OF THE YEAR (REALLY?)

FOUND YOU

(SHERYL BATES)

We know loss
Because we've felt love and hope.
We know sadness
Because we've understood happiness.
We are broken
Because we were once nearly whole.

Take comfort, dear friend.
One day in the heavens,
Away from our consciousness and earthly pain,
You'll find what you lost,
Your beloved, a part of you.

And you'll laugh with tears of joy.
Take comfort, dear friend.
You cannot find what you haven't lost.

Our first year without HGLD was a helter-skelter, bumpy ride with blindfolds on, no map, no satellite navigation, and running on fumes. We knew all the 'firsts' would be difficult, strange, and emotional. But we only knew it theoretically. We had been told what to expect by countless people, half of whom had lost someone and therefore knew from experience the trials that laid ahead, and half who didn't but were reaching for something wise, helpful, and empathetic to say.

Oh, it's your first Christmas/Hanukkah/Eid/Diwali/
Birthday/Anniversary without him,
it's going to be really difficult for you. How will you get through it?

Each one of these, and all the other, special dates are a stark reminder that *they* are not here.

You may also have heard from your friends, family, leaflets, and articles about grief and many other sources that the first year will be the hardest and most traumatic. You might be finding or have already found that to be painfully true. However, an important thing to keep in mind about the *'firsts'* is that while you will undoubtedly still love, miss, and grieve for your *'HGLD,'* managing those feelings that rise up, and sometimes threaten to overpower you, *will* become easier over time. You *will* feel stronger and more resilient as you move forward.

Part of you most likely understands and accepts that it's realistic, pragmatic, and abundantly obvious that hitting all the big, important, significant dates such as birthdays, anniversaries, or festive celebrations, particularly for the first time is going to be emotional, turbulent, and potentially daunting. In many ways it's good to be forewarned, to preempt these expected low points, and to know that when you hit those particular dates and times, it's predictable and understandable to feel your low emotions swell up and around you. Recognizing that you may need some extra self-care or support from friends and family in advance of these *'firsts'* can offer you the opportunity to plan ahead of time to be around people who care for and about you. The support and love of others will help you to get through those difficult times.

While it's helpful to be aware of and plan for the support you need to get through your *'firsts,'* it's also important not to set an expectation of a specific timeline or duration for your grief. Setting such an expectation can have the powerful though unwanted effect of priming you to be sad in advance or even to feel guilty if you aren't particularly low when you expected yourself to be. The anticipation of tracking to a particular grieving timeline might prompt you to put a reminder of how you believe you should feel into your mental calendar with a virtual, loud, and recurring reminder bell, lest you somehow forget to feel especially low on those days. Instead, allow yourself the flexibility and permission to feel what you feel, when you feel it, without recrimination. Consider how you would encourage someone else you care about and who is grieving a great loss from *their* life to be kinder and more patient with themselves. Offer yourself that same understanding, tolerance, and advice.

In all likelihood the *'firsts'* will be tough. You will reminisce. You may lament. You might wish for things to be very different. You may shed a gentle sprinkling or a broken, gushing hydrant of heartbreaking tears at those 'firsts' and many other times between them. You may doubt your ability to ever get through the dark and grungy swamps of grief and into the fresh and promising green pastures of Acceptance. But you *can* do this. You, amazing you who your 'HGLD' loved so dearly, will make it through the *'firsts'* and into the seconds and thirds. This survival instinct that is already deeply embedded within you requires a *healthy dose of endurance* to fortify you.

Over time you will begin to acknowledge that, as difficult as it has been to accept that your loved one has gone, as much as you may have been reluctant to come to terms with a new life without them physically there with you, you have amazing coping skills. You *have survived*. Perhaps not always grateful. Not always happy. But sometimes. And then, ever so gradually, more and more frequently.

After existing in our family bubble of stress and loss in Ireland for nearly five months as Dad gradually let go and left us, by the time Gina and I arrived home in the UK and Mum started to get to grips with life on her own in Ireland, we each found ourselves smack-dab in the middle of the run-up to Christmas. It sounds ridiculous to say that it was shocking for us, but it was.

The whole world was busily, happily, and colorfully decorating trees, hanging lights, sending cards, buying gifts, arranging celebrations; yet it was all made more difficult the year COVID-19 hit as it held all our togetherness hostage. The rest of the world didn't seem to realize I had lost HGLD. It was unsettling, confusing, and disorienting how, just as I found myself stuck in treacle and devoid of any notion to celebrate, life was continuing on around me, as if nothing had happened. And it wasn't only that life was 'business as usual' for everyone else. Christmas was a poignant milestone that neither Mum, Gina, nor I wanted to face. *It was Dad's favorite time of year.*

To say that he loved Christmas would be a drastic understatement. For Dad, it was never too early in the year to start watching Christmas movies and singing festive carols. Facing this without him, well, quite frankly, we all wished we could squeeze our eyes shut for a few magical seconds and know that when we opened them, we would have safely exited the booby-trapped assault course of Christmas safely, unscathed, and without having to endure the festivities. We didn't want twinkling trees, glittery cards bearing "Season's greetings," roast turkey with all the trimmings, and we certainly didn't want gifts. There was only one gift we wanted — Dad to be with us — and as that wasn't possible, nothing else would do. I felt like crying out: "*Just wake me up when it's all over.*"

Gina and I had planned to travel back to Ireland to spend a twinkle-and-turkey-free Christmas with Mum, who had booked us into a hotel for a week so we could all avoid any semblance of the usual family festivities and the achingly obvious gap left by the absence of Dad's huge, happy, and festively aproned presence. Hourly we watched for updates on the imminently expected COVID-19 travel restrictions which hovered like a dark and threatening cloud with the power to stop us, quite literally, in our tracks from traveling to Ireland. And, then, at the very last minute, a day or two before we were due to hit the road to hunker down together as a family and ride this *first* of the major *firsts* out, the cloud we had feared descended. Travel was forbidden. We were devastated. We couldn't get to Mum and she couldn't get to us.

The fact that it was entirely and absolutely outside our realm of control didn't stop us from feeling terrible that Mum was left to wake up on her own to the quietest house she had ever experienced on Christmas morning. However, we were infinitely grateful that there were lots of family members living near her and that they checked in on her during the day and sent delicious homemade dinners. But this *first* was undeniably a trial by fire.

Next came the New Year. A time entirely synonymous with hope, dreams, desires, positivity, plans, promises, celebrations, and fresh starts. Trouble was, we didn't want this fresh start. Nope. No, thank you very much. Not ready. Not yet. We'll have the old year back please! That thought only lasted until we considered what the previous year held; the pain both physical and emotional, stress, confusion, desperation, loss, and grief. As much as we knew we didn't want and weren't ready for a fresh and shiny new year of positivity, high energy, and amazing plans to be made and brought to fruition, we also couldn't have wished to relive the previous year again. Not for Dad's sake and not for ours.

So, as if we had any say in the matter, the New Year started. Fireworks lit up our windows and the dark sky above with the multicolored, vibrantly exploding excitement of hopeful revelers. The New Year arrived with a bang for many, but for us it came with a downhearted melancholy.

In retrospect, perhaps that melancholy had a reluctant whiff of an infinitesimal iota of relief. Relief that Dad would not suffer for even another moment. Relief that the previous year was over. Relief that we wouldn't have to go through all the turmoil again. Relief that Christmas was done and we had almost 12 whole months to get our heads in the game before it would come around again. Relief that the New Year festivities were popping their last corks and launching their final missiles of colorful hope skyward. Relief that we might return to some kind of adapted but doable normal. Relief that we had survived these milestone *firsts*.

As I look back at how Mum, Gina, and I had carefully, though ultimately futilely, planned a 'Christmas-free Christmas' together in Ireland to support and care for eachother, complete with all forms of non-festive food, drinks, and activities, I can now see how we were oscillating between the Denial and Anger stages of grief.

Denial: We were proactively avoiding engaging in any activities that could possibly fall under the sparkly umbrella of Christmas. We were numb, as if paralyzed by the omission of Dad in this annual celebration of family which he loved so dearly. We were struggling to process how to even *do* Christmas without him up front and center.

Anger: We each experienced our share of frustration, irritation, sadness, and hurt at the barefaced cheek of Christmas to proceed in his absence. We understood logically that it would; that others wanted, deserved, and would ensure they had a lovely time with trees, lights, gifts, decadent foods, and family surrounding them, at least as much as possible with the pandemic restrictions many countries, including England and Ireland, were enduring. But, when adrift in grief, logic has a tendency to miraculously evaporate and, like a faint mist, disappear out the wide-open windows of our hearts and minds.

It's often been said that in a war between logic and emotion... emotion will win every time. I have found this saying, particularly while grieving the loss of Dad, to be sadly true. I understand fully the logic that he just couldn't carry on, that his body and mind were spent, that he had died and that all was as it needed to be. My emotions on the other hand were more conflicted, unpredictable, and seemed to have an ability to grab me and carry me away to float down the stream of grief.

You also might identify with the ability of your emotions to overrule and stamp all over *your* logic. You may have encountered, through your loss and also at other times of your life, the war between the logic of what you know to be right or true and the emotions which pull you in an entirely different and frequently less empowering direction.

But as Elisabeth Kübler-Ross has reasoned, these phases of grief and the emotions and reactions they extract from you are important methods of self-protection. Allowing yourself time for the harsh reality to sink and settle into place. Only allowing yourself to deal with what you are capable of at any time.

Our first Christmas without Dad was undeniably difficult. Not only did we survive that 'first,' but we also got through my 50th birthday in January, then Mum's 75th birthday in early March, which was quickly followed by what would have been Dad's 80th birthday. We got through Easter, which had traditionally been a much anticipated family gathering opportunity for us, then Father's Day and Gina's birthday in June. Gradually, we were learning how to lean in, get through, and come out the other side of these firsts, knowing or perhaps believing that next time around they will be a little easier. They *are*.

As you face and steadily work your way through your first, second, third, and many more instances of all the important dates and celebrations you loved to share with *your* 'HGLD,' you will increasingly see and feel your survival instinct come to the fore. As it does, you will begin to take comfort from the memories of the special times you shared together and from the support, love, and friendship of those around you today.

These milestone *'firsts'* are not only markers of what and who you miss. They *were* and they *are* vital celebrations of the love, happiness, connections, luck, and blessings in your life.

"Life is like riding a bicycle.

To keep your balance you must keep moving."

ALBERT EINSTEIN

BABY STEPS

Your life has changed, indisputably, and in order to regain your balance and strength, you have to change, grow, and adapt with it.

None of us have the power to stop the hands of time so the *firsts* will, indeed, come around.

You may find it helpful, comforting, and even something of a stress reliever to plan how you would like to tackle all your *'firsts'* and perhaps even seconds or thirds.

This is also a great opportunity to plan little or big memorials. These could entail a gathering of friends and family to reminisce, an outing to a favorite and significant location, making something such as a Christmas tree ornament, cooking their favorite meal, baking their favorite cookies or cake, or engaging in some volunteering work at a charity you or your loved one supported or cared about.

Planning my *Firsts*, Seconds, and Thirds

Here's what to do:

1. First, identify what the special dates are. These could be birthdays (yours, theirs, your children's, etc.), anniversaries, typical times you had family gatherings, religious festivals, and so on.

2. Then think about what you might want to do to honor that relationship.

3. Also think about what you will do for *you*. Your loved one will have wanted only the best for you so, if you are struggling to figure out how to think about what you want, you can also think about what they would have wanted you to do. This could be as simple as cooking the meal you always wanted but they didn't like (extra chilies, pineapple on your pizza, escargot), or perhaps

something on a grander scale like planning a trip that you had longed to make but didn't get the chance.

Special Dates	What I want to do to honor my loved one	What I want to do for me
Example: Christmas Day	Take a trip to Wexford (where Dad came from) and visit family and friends there	Bake with cinnamon and put nutmeg into the cheese sauce for the roasted cauliflower and leeks (Dad hated any spices)

Through this exercise you can plan how to honor both your loved one and yourself. Proactively planning these life events will give you a feeling of control and balance just when you need it.

Create Your Own Uplifting Playlist

When you need a little boost or sprinkle of happiness, whether it's to help you deal with your 'firsts' or to get you going in the right direction every day, you might just find that listening to some carefully selected music is exactly what you need in those moments.

Think about what songs make you feel happy; the ones you find yourself singing or humming along to, the ones that make you smile and step a little lighter. Create your own playlist on your smartphone, computer, or other smart device at home. Alternatively, you can also generally find pretty much every song imaginable sitting available and waiting for you to listen to or watch on YouTube™.

Here's a list of some happy and uplifting songs to get you started but you can personalize this to curate your own list of heart-swelling tunes.

- Imagine (John Lennon)
- Girl on Fire (Alicia Keys)
- I'm Every Woman (Chaka Khan or Whitney Houston)
- I'm a Survivor (Destiny's Child)
- Respect (Aretha Franklin)
- Firework (Katy Perry)
- Fighter (Christina Aguilera)
- Run the World (Girls) (Beyonce)
- Roar (Katy Perry)
- Perfect (Pink)
- Feeling Good (Nina Simone or Muse)
- Happy (Pharrell Williams)
- You Gotta Be (Des'ree)
- Beautiful Day (U2)

- Raindrops Keep Fallin' on My Head (BJ Thomas or Burt Bacharach)
- Always Look on the Bright Side of Life (Monty Python's Life of Brian)
- Born Free (Matt Monro)
- I Am What I Am (Gloria Gaynor or Shirley Bassey)
- You Get What You Give (New Radicals)
- Let It Be (The Beatles)
- Heroes (David Bowie)
- I Can See Clearly Now (Johnny Nash)
- Somewhere Over the Rainbow (Israel 'IZ' Kamakawiwo'ole)

You will find that listening to happy, up-tempo, and positive-themed music will lift your energy and mood, giving you the spark you need, just when you need it.

Ultimately, it's key to remember that these times, which are an important rite of passage through grief, *will* pass. You *will* survive them. It *will* get easier.

CHAPTER 11:

DIPPING A TOE IN THE POOL OF THE FUTURE

IT'S A LONG WAY

WILLIAM STANLEY BRAITHWAITE

It's a long way the sea-winds blow
Over the sea-plains blue,—
But longer far has my heart to go
Before its dreams come true.

It's work we must, and love we must,
And do the best we may,
And take the hope of dreams in trust
To keep us day by day.

It's a long way the sea-winds blow—
But somewhere lies a shore—
Thus down the tide of Time shall flow
My dreams forevermore.

There are many things in life that I have come to realize I have no control over. Things such as my height, the weather, the actions of other people, criticism and judgment from others, the past, losing HGLD, and continuing life without his physical presence. When it comes to these things, I accept my lack of control. Other things, not so much.

You will undoubtedly, in much the same way, have come up against things in life that you couldn't control, which left you frustrated, reeling, deeply unsettled, and feeling out of your element.

Yet, if you were to really consider each of those uncontrollable circumstances in life more fully, closely, and honestly, you would realize that there are aspects of every one of them that *you can control*, each to a greater or lesser degree. Identifying the aspects you can influence just requires thinking a little differently and from an *'I can'* rather than an *'I can't'* perspective. Breaking each uncontrollable situation down into its subcomponents will make it easier to identify the attributes you can influence. Let's call that your sphere of influence or control. This approach will empower you with the spirit, grit, and determination to do the necessary; seize the control that you do have, and take the appropriate actions to influence the outcome.

When reeling from loss and grief, a frequent response is to feel out of control and powerless which results in being more susceptible to anxiety and depression. However, finding even the smallest areas that you have control over and taking the necessary action to exert your influence there can create welcome positive shifts in how you think and feel. So much so that this can quickly become a motivating new habit that you won't want to let go of.

For example, on first reflection of my 'uncontrollables,' which are listed in the first paragraph, each appears to be something over which I have absolutely no control. Here is how I could reframe them to find my sphere of influence or control.

What I can't control	What I can influence or control
My height	How I hold myself tall, whatever my height. How I value myself as lovable and perfect at being me just as I am. My weight — being at what I feel is an appropriate weight for my frame will make me feel and probably look taller.
The weather	What I wear. What I plan to do in order to maximize sun or rain. How I consider both the rain and the sun to have vital roles for me and the planet.
The actions of others	Accepting that the actions of others are outside of my control. Focusing on being accountable for my own actions and leaving others to deal with theirs.
Criticism and judgment from others	Realize that the critical people in my life are fighting their own demons and shortcomings. Know that it's not about me. Choose not to let it in. Nobody can make me agree with them other than *me*. Choose to surround myself with kind, supportive, loving people. Be completely accountable for what I believe about me. Talk to myself with the love and respect I would have for someone I care greatly for.
The past	Turning regrets into learnings. To not repeat my mistakes. Taking accountability for my choices and actions. Choosing not to be tough on myself about the past.
Losing HGLD	Knowing that I did all I could to help and care for him and spend time with him when I could.
Continuing life without HGLD	Honoring him by living a good and happy life. Keeping all our shared memories safe and freely available for me to recall and enjoy. Endowing every day with the blessings of the lessons he taught me.

The skill of identifying and reclaiming your control is a total game changer in every aspect of life. It's a skill that enables you to see possibilities where, for many people, none exist. This dramatically changes for the better not only your outcome in that situation but, most critically, your outlook on life. I can wholeheartedly vouch for embracing this mentality of seeking out and focusing on the aspects within your sphere of influence or control then taking action. I have seen the huge difference doing this makes in people's lives. Many of my coaching and hypnotherapy clients have found that embracing and making this exercise a regular habit has given them a new, empowering, and liberating lease of life.

As you adopt this energizing and compelling skill of finding your sphere of influence and control, you will notice that your ability to reframe a situation and identify the parts of it that you can actually do something about gradually comes more naturally to you. Additionally, giving yourself permission to *accept and let go* of what you cannot control provides a gentle release from carrying an emotional burden that is not yours to carry. These *two heaping spoonfuls of strength* are available to you right now.

The ability to first recognize and then reclaim your control is one of the most powerful ways you can inch toward the relief of the truthful perspective you are allowing to settle within you. When you make that galvanizing shift in how you approach and actively engage in life, you welcome the cathartic acceptance of what you can and cannot control along with a host of new and powerful feelings sparked by your readiness to take action.

Acceptance is the solid ground where many people who are grieving the loss of a loved one begin to find some release from the remorse or anxiety of what they couldn't control. Acceptance offers balance in your thoughts, emotions, and actions, the space for the belief, and the resourcefulness to carry on in life knowing that, despite your loss, the *Love Remains*.

Embracing *Acceptance* of what has gone and is now unchangeable has the power to release you from the chains of despair and hopelessness. Acceptance of what you can't influence and are willing to let go of or leave in the hands of whatever higher force you believe in, be it God, The Universe, or your own inner moral compass, can offer you the peace of mind and comfort you need and deserve, especially now. Acceptance of what you actually can influence, here, now, and in the future can fuel the *Baby Steps* that will build your resilience, confidence, and sense of purpose in life again. Through this *Acceptance* and accountability for what you can influence and control, you can begin to consider that not only does the future exist for you but that *you want and need to play an active and conscious role in it* because of the immense and heartening benefits you will feel. The role you play in life going forward, how it affects you and those around you, is up to you and within your control. You deserve this boost of morale and, in all likelihood, this is also what *your* 'HGLD' would want for you too.

Venturing forward into the future with or without our loved one entails four factors. The first three of these we are in control of and the fourth, far much less so. These four factors are:

- *Your intention or willingness to participate in life* — this is a mindset or agreement you make with yourself, eg. "I am going to join my friends for our regular meetup because I know it will be good for me to get out and be with other people."

- *Your ability, skills, or tools that help you to participate* — these are the things you leverage or do to engage with others, eg. listening to others, asking for help, engaging in conversation, feeling and showing empathy for others, and establishing and maintaining relationships.

- *Your actions* — the active steps you take to move forward, eg. going for a walk in the park, making eye contact and smiling at people you pass by, accepting invitations to events or gatherings.

- *Time* — the passage of time and how we choose to use and value our time, eg. time is one of the most fundamental measurements of life; years, months, weeks, days, minutes, moments, and it allows us to track our progress through life and to differentiate between different episodes in our life and how we feel about them.

While it might not always feel like it, we each get to decide the degree to which we are willing, the ability, skills, and tools we have or choose to develop and the actions we will take to engage in life from one day to the next. These are aspects that are, to greater or lesser degrees, within our control. However, the factor of time, like a strict but loving guardian, will take care of making sure the future happens, regardless of our willingness or lack thereof. While the progression of time is outside of your control, what you decide to do with your time is certainly within your control.

Consciously being accountable for your willingness to engage in life today and in the future, being responsible for developing and using your abilities, skills, or tools, and the actions you take are vital because these dictate the experience you have as you move into and through the future. Whether you experience sadness, how much sadness, the length, depth, shape and recurrence of your sadness, or happiness, love, hope, joy, and all the many other flavors and complexity of your emotions. Those three factors have enormous influence over how you experience your life. And *you* have enormous influence and control over those three factors and how you choose to use them to enhance your experience of life.

When considering what tools, approaches, and support her clients most frequently found helpful in coming to terms with their loss and reengaging with life, Charlene Ray has found that many accredited their strength and willingness to joining support groups or simply talking with a trusted friend. They often noted that they gained the most from the conversations and time with those who didn't try to 'fix' them or make their pain go away, but who would just sit with them and listen. Many were relieved to learn more about grief, enough to know that what they were going through was normal, to be expected, and that they were doing it exactly right for them. Charlene often encourages her clients to spend time in nature and to embrace self-compassion, which helps them to feel supported and teaches them how to be kinder to themselves. As they began to move forward, some embarked on sizable life changes such as moving house, changing jobs or entire careers, writing a book, starting a foundation, or teaching their knowledge or skills to others. Some told her that even through their loss and grief they found new meaning in life. Most, she is happy to share, find their way and, in doing so, discover laughter and joy again.

As Pat Labez sought inspiration, motivation, and momentum to push forward again in life after the loss of her sister Joy, she took some sessions with a tae kwon do Master. These physically cathartic sessions helped her to release physical blocks and allowed her body to 'flow' and move again. She also took health supplements which aided in lifting the grief brain fog as well as offering her body a much-appreciated health boost. Above all, for Pat, it was *action* that helped her to edge forward, onward, and upward. She found that inactivity promoted depression, whereas, positive activity, measurable accomplishments, and surrounding herself with good, positive, loving people helped combat her grief. What Pat has learned from her journey through grief to Acceptance is to truly embrace life and the little sparkles we often miss, and to simply be more aware and appreciative of the daily miracles all around her.

For Esther, connecting with others who had also lost someone special helped her to know that they got through it and, therefore, she could too. In particular, two colleagues at work who had each lost their wives in unrelated situations sat down for a coffee with her. Esther found their chat very reassuring and it reinforced that she could and *would* get through the loss of Matt. Just getting on with everyday life helped her greatly. Often she found herself thinking, "Oh, I shouldn't be doing this," about simple everyday things, expecting herself to instead be focused on grieving. But then, she would wonder, "What would Matt say? Would he be okay with this?" For example, a few months after he died, Esther found herself conflicted by the need to take a business trip to Budapest. It was all still so raw and painful that she wasn't sure what to do. But when she wondered what Matt would say, instantly she knew without any hesitation that he would say "Go!" So she did. It was a bittersweet experience as many of our future experiences without our loved ones will be. Esther recalls so clearly stepping into the beautiful hotel room with incredible views across the historic and stunning city and crying because she knew he would have loved it. But through this journey and life's assorted travails, she has come to realize that she is tough, in control, resilient, and a natural survivor.

As she came to terms with her loss, engaged in the present, and began planning for the future, what Gina found helpful and comforting was talking with family and friends. She also found it helpful to practice a little mindfulness. Looking at photos and videos. Listening to her Pappy's voice. Immersing herself in nature. Enjoying the vibrant life and hope to be found in her garden with the shades and blooms of all seasons and the birds that visit for a while, then flutter away for an adventure, but always returning to brighten her day again. And spending time with her sister *(love you Sis xxx)* recalling happier times and memories as well as making new happy memories through new experiences shared over coffees, chats, giggles, and planning exciting adventures together.

The immensity of this learning experience has made Gina more aware of her own mortality and, funnily enough, less afraid of the 'after' bit now that she knows her Pappy will be there waiting with open arms when it's her *time*.

Gina's advice to anyone coming to terms with loss is to talk. Talk to your family, friends, colleagues, even strangers. People are, on the whole, wonderful, caring, empathetic, and willing to listen. You will find it feels a little easier each time you talk about your loved one. She also encourages taking time for yourself. Do kind things for yourself. Take time to think about happy memories and to bring your focus back to those happier moments. She urges you not to expect too much, too soon but to set yourself small, achievable targets. Her final nugget of wisdom for you is, if you find you are being drawn into melancholy thoughts, focus on three happy words you associate with your loved one, or on three things you love about what they taught you. Great advice indeed.

Ciara has realized that if she could get through the loss of her friend Tom as a teenager then she can get through anything as long as she is patient with herself and her emotions. Learning the importance of allowing time for her personal journey without comparison or expectation has opened her up to healing and moving forward again to live her life. Understanding what she *can* control and accepting what happened has made her wiser. More balanced. More accepting. More at peace with herself.

Mum has recognized that it helps to stay busy and, as she loves to keep her house impeccably tidy and beautifully decorated, she is never short of tasks to occupy her. Most days she goes to the pretty local park for a walk in nature and never fails to be uplifted by the outing. The quietness of the house can be very unsettling and lonely, but Mum has good friends and wonderful family who keep in touch with her constantly by text, phone, and video calls. Even a simple trip to do the grocery shopping lifts her spirits and gets her out and among the busy hubbub of people. These connections with others are a vital support that are building her fortitude and ability to accept each day as it comes.

Charlene and her clients, Pat, Esther, Gina, Ciara, and Mum have each tapped into their varying and gradually increasing measures of willingness to participate in life. They have also employed a wide selection of tools, skills, and actions that have aided them in finding their inner strength, momentum, and sheer will to, bit by bit, get back to feeling more like themselves again. Perhaps an altered version of themselves, without the loved one they still love and miss, but definitely stronger and little by little more positive, courageous, and feisty. They have each seen and felt the difference that the passage of time can make. They learned to be patient and gentle with themselves and to allow their journey through grief to be *their journey*, on their terms, and in their time.

If you are not yet as far along the journey as Charlene, her clients, Pat, Esther, Gina, Ciara, or Mum, know that it's okay. You may not yet be feeling as resilient or positive as they are. Give yourself permission to do this *your way* and *in your time*. You will get there, into a stronger place within you, at your speed. Tell yourself now, "It's okay for me to do this my way and at my speed." Be patient, kind, and gentle with yourself. Know that just reading the stories and experiences of others in this book is beginning or continuing your journey back to feeling more like you again. You *will* get there.

When it comes to finding the reasons, resources, and resilience to engage in life after loss, some common themes emerge from the journeys, stories, and learnings of others who have traveled this same painful and rocky road before. As they unfolded their own unique journeys through grief, many have found that focusing on what they could control, accepting what they couldn't control, taking action regularly, being kind, patient, and loving to themselves, and spending time outdoors in nature have all made their loss more bearable and their life ahead more engaging, positive, and joyful.

One of the most simple, achievable, and uplifting ways you can take regular action is by going outside and being in nature. Luckily, for most people, getting out into nature, whether that's your garden, a local park, a nearby forest or beach, or even a city street lined with pretty trees under the expansive canopy of the ever changing sky, is within their control.

There are a number of solid and well-documented benefits to spending time regularly in nature. Many studies on the effects of being outdoors, particularly in a green environment, have shown a substantial reduction in fear, anger, stress, and the symptoms of depression, even reducing blood pressure, heart rate, muscle tension, and stress hormones. These studies also revealed a significant improvement in mood and self-esteem, with super boosts in the feel-good hormones. The color green is widely known to make us feel optimistic and refreshed and symbolizes health, springtime, freshness, renewal, and hope.

Have you ever hugged a tree? If you have then you may have noticed that this simple, abundant, and free activity increases the levels of oxytocin, serotonin, and dopamine, a wonderful natural cocktail that helps us to feel calm, connected, peaceful, and happy, even boosting our immune system and overall well-being. As if that wasn't enough to sell you on the benefits of a quick tree hug, they also naturally remove carbon dioxide and other nasties such as pollution and other harmful substances from the air and in turn supply us with pure, fresh oxygen. So the next time you stand under a tree, don't forget to breathe and enjoy the finest air nature can provide. Go on, cast aside any notion of embarrassment and hug a tree today.

Accepting what you can and what you can't control, being active and taking action, whether those actions are big or small, and going outdoors and spending a little time in nature will each play a vital role in shifting your mood and emotions in the right direction. Your ability to take action reveals and taps into your baked-in-at-birth unconquerable spirit and desire to survive. The results will include an increase in your confidence and self-esteem and setting you on the path to moving on with life, whether one step, one minute, one day, or one plan at a time. So, give yourself permission right now to gently dip your toe in the pool of the future.

"I am tomorrow, or some future day, what I establish today.
I am today what I established yesterday or some previous day."

JAMES JOYCE

BABY STEPS

Life may have thrown you a curve ball of immense proportions but you have already proven that you are amazing and you are a survivor.

As you begin to move forward and dip your toe in the pool of the future, do so slowly at first and always at your own pace. Know that continuing on with your life despite the pain of your loss is inevitable, not optional, and it's what your loved one undoubtedly wants for you.

Here's what to do:

1. What Your Loved One Wants for You

Before he passed, the husband of iconic British TV presenter Esther Rantzen left clear instructions that when he was gone, she should put a little grove of trees and a seat on the hill behind their house so he could lovingly keep an eye on her. What a sweet sentiment and a lovely way to honor each other.

Think about what *your 'HGLD'* would want or ask you to do after they passed. It's possibly fair to say that they sometimes knew and understood you and your needs even better than you did. Listen to their wishes for you. Be guided by them, their love, and their good intentions for you.

What my loved one wanted for me	What I will do
Example: To ensure I was surrounded by family	• Plan a trip to spend a week with my sister/brother/daughter/son • Arrange a weekly video catch-up with my family • Arrange a regular monthly dinner, rotating around the various family homes

What my loved one wanted for me	What I will do

You may find this exercise is particularly helpful in offering you a little perspective and balance as it encourages you to set aside notions of guilt that you may have harbored about carrying on with life after your loss. You will find it comforting to embrace the guidance of your 'HGLD,' knowing that they want what's best for you.

2. What I Can't and What I Can Control

Earlier in this chapter we looked at how helpful and empowering it can be to look at the things that appear to be outside of your control with a new perspective and the objective of identifying what aspect of that situation is actually within your control.

Where possible, identify the aspect that is within your control and consider what action you can and are willing to take with this new perspective.

Here's what to do:

1. Make a list of the things or situations you feel you are not in control of. These are often the things that make you feel helpless, frustrated, unsettled, or even keep you awake at night.

2. Then consider each of those 'uncontrollables' and search for what aspect of or around each one you can either influence to some degree *or* control. It may not be that you can control the entire situation but you will probably find some aspect of it that you can influence.

3. Finally, once you have identified the things you can influence or control, decide what action you need to take in order to utilize your influence and feel the benefit.

What I can't control	What I can influence or control	What action I can take
Example: Losing HGLD	Knowing that I did all I could to help him and spend time with him when I could.	Let go of any guilt regarding HGLD's death

Through this exercise you may surprise yourself to find that when you reframe a difficult situation, it radically changes your perspective or ability to recognize and reclaim your control. When you break down a difficult situation into these components, you can give yourself permission to let go of and accept the aspects you cannot control. That alone offers considerable consolation and liberation from anxiety, stress, and frustration. Through this exercise you can also, instead of believing the entire situation to be unmanageable and overpowering, identify the things you *have* influence over and empower yourself to restore some control in your life. This skill is one of the most empowering and confidence-building gifts you can give yourself.

3. Embrace Your Own Words of Love, Resilience, and Strength

Now, as you have learned a little more about the importance of treating yourself gently and choosing to recognize and accept what is and what is not within your control, this is the ideal time to revisit the exercise on *'Seizing Control of My Thoughts and Words'* that we covered in Chapter 4. This exercise was all about learning to talk to and about yourself the way you would talk to or about someone you love or respect greatly.

Take some time to look back at what you captured in that template and consider if your words are serving you well and treating you with love and kindness.

You might also want to start a new list here.

Here's what to do:

1. Firstly, review what you captured when you did this *'Baby Steps'* exercise in Chapter 4. Consider if the content is still relevant or perhaps needs to be updated, amended, or added to in order to reflect your current limiting language or inner dialogue.

2. Use the left side of the template to capture the hurtful, harmful, unsupportive words and thoughts that are building

hurtful, harmful, and unsupportive beliefs, habits, and feelings. These are the things you hear yourself think, say, or perhaps even do which make you unhappy or bring you down. Then, for each of the hurtful beliefs you have listed, on the right side of the template capture the kind, caring, supportive, strengthening, and loving words you would use to establish new, kinder, and better beliefs. It's okay if you don't yet believe or feel them; you have yet to build that muscle by using those words. It's important here to only describe what you want to say, feel, and believe rather than what you no longer want to say, feel, or believe.

3. If you are struggling to find nice things for the right side, think about what you would say to support someone you care greatly for.

4. Choose to stop saying the hurtful things on the left. When you hear them pop into your head or come out of your mouth, choose to say, "That's not me. I don't say that anymore."

5. Choose to be kind to yourself. Start saying the new words from the right side all the time. Begin by reading them to yourself from the list (only the right side!) 10-12 times each day, and do it without counterbalancing those wonderful words and thoughts with any notion of not feeling or believing it yet or that it's not true. You are only now starting to program them into your brilliant mind and it needs clarity and consistency. The beliefs and the feelings to match the words *will* follow.

Old outdated hurtful, harmful, unsupportive words, thoughts, and beliefs	New words to create new kind, caring, supportive, strengthening, and loving beliefs *(what you want, not what you don't want)*
Examples: I am alone	I am blessed to have family and friends who care for and support me I am resilient and am doing brilliantly, HGLD would be so proud of me
I feel broken	I am strong I am getting stronger every day
I can't cope	I have amazing coping skills I know how to love and care for myself

As you may have found from the previous time you did this exercise in Chapter 4, when you consciously choose your words carefully and begin to talk to yourself with great care, love, and respect, you open yourself up to healing, love, life, and resilience. *Embracing Your Own Words of Love, Resilience, and Strength* on a continual basis will make this vital skill feel not only natural to you but also critical in how you feel about all aspects of your day-to-day life.

4. Write a Letter to Your Loved One:

Being ready to dip your toe in the pool of the future can become a more welcome and doable prospect when you feel you have had the opportunity to say the things that are being held inside your head or heart, but have not yet or sufficiently been aired. The catharsis you can experience when you have given your deepest thoughts a voice, whether in conversation or on paper, is hearteningly soothing and another positive and active step in the direction of achieving Acceptance.

Using the template below, your favorite notepaper, a lined notepad, a page of photocopy paper, or even your electronic device of choice, begin to write a letter to your loved one that has passed. Tell them what you miss about them and what you love about them, learned from them, and are grateful for. Tell them how you will share the treasured gifts they gave you onward to others and what you are doing that you know would make them proud of you.

Date: _____

Dear _____,

With love,

_____

Sometimes, capturing our thoughts and words physically on paper provides a little clarity, comfort, and connection. Put your letter in a safe place and consider writing another one to them when you are a little further along your path of healing.

5. Go Out Into Nature

If you want a change in your feelings, particularly for the better, you need to make a change in your physiology.

Go for a walk in a park or in the woods. Plant your bare feet in the grass. Sit or walk by the water. Listen for the birds. Sit and be still and present in nature.

Hug a tree. Don't be shy, lots of people do it. Find a beautiful, growing, live tree and wrap your arms around the life force of its trunk. Just let your thoughts disappear for a minute or two. Breathe. You might feel light-headed with all that super pure oxygen!

Allow all those feel-good hormones to do their thing.

Now you are truly and lovingly dipping your toe in the pool of the future.

And, it's okay.

CHAPTER 12:

REALITY CHECK

"Since we cannot change reality, let us change the eyes which see reality."

NIKOS KAZANTZAKIS

The majority of this book has focused with purpose and intention on dealing with the loss of someone you love and miss greatly. Perhaps even wholeheartedly, absolutely, unreservedly, and unconditionally.

However, even in my relationship with HGLD, there were occasional times when he was less HGLD (remember that means **H**andsome **G**od-**L**ike **D**ad) and more of a tough-love, rule-enforcing, my-way-or-the-highway, 'Type A' kind of Dad. Our relationship wasn't always perfect, at least not every single day. There were times, thankfully not many, when the red mist of abstract anger would descend, and he would flip into 'warrior defender of his queen' mode. Generally, this only happened when he thought that Mum was upset. That was the only red rag to his inner raging bull.

He was, as you have read and perhaps conjured the image in your own mind from my raw and open insight into his life, in the majority of situations, a twinkly-eyed, smiling, chortling, mischievous, good-natured, and gentle giant.

Regardless of my unshakeable ability to commit to unequivocally adore and have stars in my eyes for Dad, I also recognize that he was a real, flawed human being. But then, so am I. He had his buttons, which when pressed, and as children we did that on occasion, unleashed a different side to him. Human. Bumpy. Sharp-edged. *Real.*

It has taken me nearly a lifetime to realize that, when it comes to our closest relationships, it's okay to be truthful to yourself, if not to others, about the reality, the ups and downs, swings, and roundabouts of even the best of relationships. Nobody is perfect. Not even HGLD. Perfection is unattainable and is an unfair and contorted work of fiction that places the object of our affection precariously on a pedestal they never requested, setting them up to fail or fall back down to us mere mortals on earth.

When you think about your own 'HGLD,' you can probably also identify with the human, imperfect side of them. The characteristics that might have led to disagreements, frustration, or heated debates.

The pursuit of perfection, whether in ourselves or in others, can lead to what's known as the halo effect. This is a distorted perception, or cognitive bias, that changes how we interpret reality and form our impressions of others. Basically, it means looking at someone through rose-tinted glasses instead of with 20:20 vision. Kind of like building them up to be a knight in shining armor, tall, toned, with a six-pack, fluent in 12 languages, an animal whisperer, capable of feats of immense strength, with the cultured sophistication of a baron, the ability to strip an engine, cook the perfect soufflé, gather you wildflowers, write poetry, and sit enthralled, gazing lovingly while listening to you talk about the argument you overheard on the train earlier that day. *Nobody* can live up to all that. It's unfair and it's unrealistic.

To acknowledge only the magically wondrous qualities of your loved one makes it incredibly difficult to cope with the loss. It means you are trying to cope with losing something and someone unrealistically and unreasonably perfect. This, in turn, can make you feel that *you* never matched up, *you* are or were not good enough, *you* are broken and that the praise, love, and acceptance you enjoyed in that relationship will never exist again. All these untruths can result from an utopian and skewed perception of other people's perfection. *Nobody* is perfect.

Sometimes people grieve the passing of a parent, partner, or other pivotal figure in their life who wasn't even kind or loving to them. You might ask how or why they would grieve such a loss. They are, in that case, most likely grieving for the love, acceptance, or praise that they never received. The missed opportunity to hear what they always wanted to hear and now never will.

If that's you, I am truly sorry that you were not seen, heard, or loved as you deserved to be. I want you to know that whatever love was not shown to you, that does not for even a moment mean, nor has it ever meant that you are not completely lovable exactly as you are. *You are.* You are enough. You have always been enough. You always will be.

So, ground yourself in reality. Realign how you feel emotionally with how that person actually was, warts and all, for better and for worse. Be honest with yourself. This realignment, truth, and clarity provides a more secure footing in our beliefs about the life we deserve and our capability to go on, to move forward, to know that we can and will get through this.

It's okay to take off the rose-tinted glasses that obscure our reality in order to see and love your special someone for who and what they were or are. Believe me, it doesn't diminish the love by even a nano-smidgen. Give them room to be or to have been human. They will repay the favor to you too. So they might be a little less knight-in-shining-armor than you might have dreamed once upon a time. That's okay.

Dad's human frailty, while it didn't bubble over often, made him real. It also serves to remind me that it's okay to be fallible, to get stuff wrong, and to not always be perfect.

I can point to a few less-than-perfect character traits about myself that probably drive my partner, my family, and perhaps my friends to distraction at times (a tendency toward perfectionism, always solving problems, managing situations, being a high achiever, yada yada yada...). But they still love me. *Exactly as I am.*

Phew! What a relief that it's okay to be human. I've got this. I *can* get through this.

So can *you*.

> *"You yourself, as much as anybody in the entire universe, deserve your love and affection."*
>
> BUDDHA

BABY STEPS

If you find yourself conflicted or confused as you grieve for someone or a relationship that didn't serve you as well as you wanted, it's time for a reality check. Painting yourself into a corner of always having to view that person or relationship as perfect will drain your energy, steal your 'spoons' *(see the 'Managing My Spoons' exercise from Chapter 1)* and build a wall between you and the love, acceptance, praise, and life you deserve.

It's okay if you don't have anything to add here but many are not so lucky.

Start here and now. Give yourself permission to be *fair, open,* and *honest.* You deserve that and it's okay. Allowing yourself this candid reality check in regard to what you wish was different about the relationship and what you would, with the benefit of experience, do differently in the future will help you to have a voice where you might not have at times in the past. It will also help you to make decisions for your future fueled by a healthy and balanced love and respect for yourself.

Here's what to do:

1. Focus on the reality of the relationship you had with the person you have in mind and how it made you feel. Consider the things you wish they did differently. These may be things that would have made you feel more loved, heard, supported, or accepted.

2. Then think about the things you always wanted and needed to hear from them but were never said or not frequently enough. It's also worth thinking about why you needed to hear those things and what hearing them would have meant to you.

3. Next, capture the things you didn't get to say to them. Perhaps you didn't get to say some of the things you really wanted and needed because you were afraid to upset or anger them or because you felt they wouldn't understand and would be hurt. Maybe you never felt you had the right or empowerment to say what you wanted. Possibly, you ran out of time before they passed or left your life. You can still find your voice, even if just by capturing it here or saying it out loud on your own or to a trusted confidant.

4. Now think about the things you wanted to do, have, or achieve with them but never did. These things may not have been important to them but were to you. Also consider why these things were important to you and what difference they would have made in your life or how you felt.

5. Finally, with that clarity of vision that comes from experience and hindsight, decide what you will do differently in the future to ensure you have power over your own life, you are seen and heard, and you have a right to feel and be safe, happy, and loved.

Time for a reality check

Things I wished they did differently	*Example:* I wish _____ had been open to hearing my thoughts and considered my opinion of value and importance.
Things I wanted to hear but didn't	What do you think we should do? Thank you. I'm sorry. You are very important to me.
What I didn't get to say to them but wanted to	Sometimes I don't feel valued by or important to you. I feel my opinion is irrelevant to you.
Things I wanted us to do but never happened	Travel to Italy together. Get a dog. Go out for dinner for quality time together.
What I will do differently in the future	Choose to focus on relationships with people who value my opinion.. Plan a trip to Italy. Find opportunities for quality time with people I love.

Things I wished they did differently		
Things I wanted to hear but didn't		
What I didn't get to say to them but wanted to		
Things I wanted us to do but never happened		
What I will do differently in the future		

The reality check and perspective you give yourself as a result of this exercise can be incredibly empowering and inspiring. By doing this you can come to know and accept that you are completely worthy of love and respect and how to be valued by those you choose to build relationships of all kinds with.

You are enough

You have always been enough

You always will be.

CHAPTER 13:

MAKING PROGRESS

THE JIGSAW

DOESITSAY

It's a box full of a broken picture.
The jigsaw of our lives,
This corner of joy, that funny-shaped bit of sorrow,
The 10,000 pieces of the times of our life
Each fitting closely together in a puzzle of moments.
It'll make sense.
Ask for help sorting the sky from the trees.
Perhaps a friend has done it before,
And if there's a piece missing, it won't matter when it's done.
You'll see the whole thing.

As with so many people who have lost someone vital to their life and happiness, the intricate, heartfelt, and unique pathway through grief that you are on is a journey, not a destination. There is no single sign or moment that will declare with flashing neon lights that you have crossed the invisible border and arrived into the fabled land of being entirely free of grief.

In truth, you may never be entirely free, and you possibly wouldn't want to be either. Most people set a goal of feeling they can cope with their loss. That they can carry on with life without the kind of sadness that makes getting through each day difficult, hollow, and painful. Many want to feel absolved of any guilt they felt about carrying on, making plans, feeling happy, and finding joy in life. None of these goals are unreasonable or unachievable. None of these wishes are things your loved one wouldn't want for you. None of these require you to be entirely free from grief. What they *do* require is *your* permission to live life in a way that allows space for the love you shared, and still remains, to exist within you. That love can and does exist within you already. Allow it some time in your thoughts. Give it a voice through your words. Hear the beautiful emotion of it when you share stories, memories, lessons, and laughter with others.

I am sure you would like to know how Charlene, Pat, Esther, Mum, Gina, and Ciara are all progressing along their own unique journeys through grief.

For Charlene, the loss of her Father at such a young age shaped her life and, interestingly, her purpose. Charlene is a grief counselor because of that loss. She did not want anyone feeling such intense grief to travel that journey alone. Her own grief has made her appreciate life more and focus on what really matters. What really matters to Charlene, what helps her most, is spending time with the people she loves, visiting the places she feels connected to, being in nature, enjoying her garden... not wasting time worrying or spending too much time in the past.

Charlene also sees a similar response in many of her clients. At some point along their path of grief, they recognize how it has changed them and how they want to live. Many make big changes like a new career, a move to another part of the world. Some start a foundation or organization. For others, it's more simple. They recognize that, for them, it's about wanting to spend time with the people they love, taking the opportunity to tell them they love them, and quite simply enjoying the beauty of life.

One of Charlene's clients who never thought a relationship would be possible after the death of their spouse found new love with a partner who had also lost their spouse. They make space for the loves that died in their life with photos and memories as they enjoy the new love and companionship they now share. Another client, who was at her mother's bedside when she died, decided after a year of grieving that she wanted to be there to help others and is now a hospice volunteer. Another who was particularly moved by poetry during her grieving process decided to compile a book of poems about grief for others to benefit from.

Sometimes comfort is found in heart-shaped rocks collected on the beach or visits by songbirds in the garden. The signs of love and connection can be very small and subtle. Charlene believes that while there is no timeline on grief, at some point there, is usually a shift as glimmers of hope increase and new meaning and purpose are found.

Charlene has found that we grow with and through our grief. We don't get over it; it lives in us and changes us. Critically, she has found that we continue to love, even though we know that we will quite possibly grieve again one day.

Where does Pat stand with her grief today? Well, interestingly enough, since her much loved sister Joy took her last breath, her New Year kickoff always involves a much deeper introspection now than in years past. Pat found Joy's four-year anniversary was particularly difficult and felt an even greater sense of loss than the three previous years. Her missing presence felt magnified by the realization of its finality. Fortunately, Pat found that having an extremely busy year with no time to dwell too much on sadness and regret, particularly the regret of not moving to Virginia, where Joy lived sooner, helped her to cope. In her thoughts she hears Joy saying, "See, Pat, you should've moved here sooner! We could've had a lot more fun!" Indeed. Pat believes her full calendar is actually one of her best coping mechanisms. Her time is filled with activities and projects she and Joy might have done together, but, certainly, she is confident it would have made Joy proud.

Since writing a moving story called "Find Joy in the Journey" in her first compilation book, *Ignite Possibilities*, Pat has had a greater sense of peace. In a somewhat unusual coincidence, Pat was recently approached by two entirely different people who felt compelled to let her know of Joy's spiritual presence, her pride in what Pat has achieved, and her encouragement to keep writing and pursuing her dreams. "Keep going," was the common thread relayed by both people. They helped her understand that living to the fullest is actually a way of honoring our loved ones who have gone before us. Pat has found great comfort in that thought.

And so, as Pat continues her journey, she is now, more than ever, con-sciously grateful for the limited time she has in this physical world. She is now also more selective about what she chooses to spend precious time and energy on.

Pat knows that grief and loneliness are very real, whatever the cause. She has found that taking action, volunteering, and being of service to others is, for her, the best therapy. Because of this, she has launched a program, "Third Act Encore." This is a global platform featuring people over the age of 50 who have transitioned to another stage of life, rein-vented themselves, and have made a difference in their communities. The program includes a streaming network, in-person and online events, and articles that provide hope, inspiration, and empowerment to restore, repurpose, and redefine retirement. It's safe to say that Pat is tapping into her empowerment and making changes that positively impact not only her, but so many other people around her.

Esther still thinks of Matt regularly. Something will pop into her head such as an experience they shared, or she finds herself saying little sayings or using words that only they would use. When Esther spends the weekend with her brother and his family, Matt's name still comes up happily in conversation. She also spends time with Matt's sister. He's still alive in her thoughts and connections, and will always be 35 in her mind while Esther and all their joint friends and family keep aging.

The experience has helped Esther to realize how precious life is, what's important and what's not important, and that things can change in the blink of an eye. She tends now to 'seize the day,' much like Pat, rather than putting off the things she has always wanted to do.

Esther is a Mum now to JJ, and considers that to be the most amazing and fulfilling role she has played. Not a day goes by without her feeling incredibly grateful for her gorgeous little boy. She also sometimes thinks about what a great Dad Matt would have been. Despite not being religious, she is pretty sure that if Matt is 'somewhere' looking down on them both, he would be happy for them. She knows from personal experience that life can sometimes be colossally tough and "rubbish." However, she fully recognizes that at other times it can also be amazing. So, Esther thanks her lucky stars daily that she and JJ have their health, each other, and wonderful friends and family. For Esther, that's all that matters, and that's also what motivates, comforts, and sparks joy for her every day.

As Mum looks back on her year of 'firsts,' she recognizes what a tough year it had been. It was a year like no other. Not only because Mum had lost the love of her life, but because of the COVID-19 pandemic, she was mostly restricted to remaining home, alone in the house they had shared together. Gradually though, as social restrictions were relaxed, she was able to get out and meet up with family and friends. This was a critical lifeline for Mum, who readily acknowledges the necessity of being around people. Particularly people who helped her to feel loved, who would chat over coffee, or visit garden centers and help her to plant flowers in the garden in memory of Dad. Now she can look forward to the colorful display that will be waiting to greet her every morning come springtime. She has shared that one of the most important things for her was to keep busy. This proved to be a key coping mechanism for her.

Twelve months after losing her Bobby, Mum realizes she is learning to survive in a different way. She carries him in her heart throughout her day and night and chats to him all the time. Just before the first anniversary of Dad's passing, Mum was invited to join several family members on a short holiday to Spain. While there, she surprised everyone by saying yes to an invitation to go on a paragliding adventure. She had so much fun and was amazed to hear herself laughing. She also joined a daily exercise class which, as it was held over live video, offered her the opportunity to not only work on her fitness and flexibility, but also to spend time with lovely, like-minded people in her age group. Many have become friends.

Some days are good, others a little less so, but she knows that she is strong and will make it through to the next good day with a little faith in herself and the love of her family and friends. It's still relatively early in Mum's journey through grief, but she is gradually building her resilience and acclimatizing to her new normal.

For Gina, as she looks back in time, the intensity of the months, weeks, and days leading up to her pappy's death culminated in the staggering reality of the most devastating loss she had ever encountered. However, on reflection, she is able to say with a good deal of certainty that she has come a great distance in her journey through grief. Some milestones weren't always obvious at the time but often noticed coincidentally. For example, for a long time after he passed, every time she woke up from sleeping, the pained and desperate image and thoughts of her precious Pappy at the end of his life were the first things on her mind. She can't say exactly when, but at some point, she realized that those thoughts were no longer the first thing on her mind upon waking and that the haunting image of him had been supplanted by the beautiful image of a smiling, happy Pappy. An image like the lovely framed photo that Mum gave to each of us, just to keep him nearby. That alone, for Gina, was a huge success and a step in a positive direction.

Now she finds she is smiling, both inside and outside when her Pappy's image comes to mind. Each little change chips away at the grief process. Almost like a bus route to recovery, or at least a new and better destination. Each positive change is like reaching the next bus stop on the journey. Gina used to see so many things around her that reminded her of the sadness she felt knowing that her Pappy was no longer a physical part of her life. She now embraces the things that remind her of him, and they fill her with happiness. Things like a song on the radio, seeing the Christmas decorations in the shops, a silly joke that he would have found hilarious, a good meal enjoyed with family and friends, and so many other simple but meaningful memories.

A year ago, Gina could never have imagined feeling happy when she saw reminders, but now she is relieved to report that *time is kind*. Every day, without fail, she gives thanks for all the things she sees, hears, smells, tastes, or touches that remind her of her Pappy. For her, it's very much a sensory journey through grief toward a new normal. Gina considers grief to be a previously unnavigable road that has no right or wrong route. Some days she might hit a roadblock or need to reroute, but as long as she is heading for the right destination, she knows she will get a little bit closer every day. Another positive lesson from grief has to be the value found in strong family bonds and good friendships. Both have helped to buoy her up on days she felt she might sink. It's equally satisfying for her to know that we have helped each other as a family through our challenging days, and she believes that good communication offers a critical lifeline.

Gina still browses through photos and video clips of her Pappy most days. These, for her, are a comfort blanket and help her to feel his presence around her each day. She acknowledges that there are, and will be, some difficult days but stresses the importance of not being afraid to call someone up and just say, "Today's not a good day." In doing this, she reaches out for the help she needs and also helps others by letting them know how much she appreciates their listening ear or kind words of comfort.

Most of all, Gina is grateful to have close family relationships, a wonderful husband and daughter, fantastic friends, and a wealth of lessons in appreciating the beauty of life around her. These lessons were often imparted by her dear Pappy. So, in acknowledging his death, and remembering his life, Gina can see that her journey to the new destination is already well underway, and she plans to use all those sensory reminders to help her navigate the remainder of that journey, for as long as it takes.

As cliché as it sounds, Ciara has found that *time really is a great healer.* It's not that she feels any differently about having lost her friend Tom or her grandfather, 'Bobbyshafto.' For her, it's more about being comfortable to a greater extent with the feelings that her loss evoked. The sadness doesn't creep up and jump out at her anymore. Neither does it cause her to stop in her tracks and burst into tears. Not anymore. Instead, what happens now that some time has passed, is that the memories and feelings associated with her loss slowly, calmly, and manageably wave over her. As they do, these memories leave the echo of a dull ache deep in the center of her chest, a lump in her throat, and misty eyes. Ciara now has a sense of warm familiarity with her grief and, ultimately, what she believes is Acceptance.

If Ciara could go back in time to when Tom died and offer some words of advice to her younger self, she would say, "Be patient with yourself." To be patient is to be kind, and, now more than ever, kindness is what she *and you* deserve.

As for me, I have learned that our loved ones, though passed, will always be with us. I can have a conversation with HGLD any time I want. All I need to do is talk about what's on my mind, and when I listen, I can hear exactly what he would say. It gives me immense comfort to know that he is still with me, in my DNA, in my personality and character, my life lessons and my choices. I was blessed to have him in my life and while I miss and think about him every day, I know that my grief has changed. It has become something more constructive, more enriching, and comforting. Something that provides greater proportions of happy memories, joy, and love than sadness.

Experiencing the loss of my treasured Dad, feeling and seeing the impact of grief on myself and other who miss him desperately, inspired me to write this book. My loss motivated me to share my experience and the experience of others in grief to help *you* through this difficult time too. To offer you a way to cope, to begin to heal, and to live again after your loss. Writing and entrusting my story and experience with you has offered me the beautiful catharsis that comes from being vulnerable, open, and honest. In turn, I truly hope it helps you on your journey of healing. You deserve that same understanding, support, and light at the end of the tunnel.

Yes, I can say that for me personally, while I still miss HGLD every day, *things are looking up.*

You may have identified with some of the stories, reactions, and feelings shared throughout this book. You may take some comfort in knowing you are not alone in your loss. I truly hope that reading this has helped and will continue to help you find your way back to the resilient, loving, lovable, brave, worthy, wonderful you who your special someone loved very much.

I hope that the sharing of deeply personal stories of others who, like you have lost someone special, the insights into how and why grief plays a vital role in adapting to your new normal, and the *'Baby Steps'* resilience-building actions at the end of each chapter have offered you some comfort, connection, inspiration, and guidance.

Take some time to review what you wrote for each 'Baby Step' exercise or, if you skipped any, go back and fill in the gaps. Doing this will gradually build your very own, personalized grief survival guide. One you can dip into on your own time, going at your pace, finding and using your own experience and words, and revisit when the notion takes you for a boost or to see what progress you are making through your grief journey.

The path you have found yourself on is evolving and will continue to evolve and eventually settle into a rhythm or new normal that *will* work for you.

Make space in your daily routine for a little self-acceptance and self-love first thing in the morning. End your day with gratitude for those little or big things you noticed, felt, or benefited from during the day. Most of all, be kind, patient, and gentle with yourself. Talk to yourself with the same love, positivity, and respect you would offer to others in your situation. These resilience-building practices are entirely within your control. These are the loving habits that will gently and gradually, day-by-day, support, strengthen, and envelop you in the knowledge that...

Love Remains.

BABY STEPS

Now that we have spent some time together and you have figured out some of your own learnings on your grieving process through the experiences and stories shared, insights into grief, and 'Baby Steps' exercises, it's time to review what you have learned and how it is going to help you.

Holding Myself Accountable

Here's what to do:

1. Below is a list of all the 'Baby Steps' exercises from each chapter of the book. Look back through your notes from when you completed the exercises and fill in the remaining blank column with how you believe each exercise *can* help you.

2. If you haven't yet completed the 'Baby Steps' exercises, consider gradually making your way through them all sequentially and at a pace that works for you, or alternatively, 'cherry-pick' the exercises you feel you are ready for.

Chpt #	Chapter Name	Baby Step Exercise	How This Can Help Me
1	Losing HGLD	Managing my spoons	
2	The Uniqueness of Grief	Create your personalized 'HGLD' acronym	
3	Grief Is a Stealthy Companion	My advice to my current-day self	
3	Grief Is a Stealthy Companion	Well-intended advice of others	
3	Grief Is a Stealthy Companion	Helping others to be better listeners	
4	The Unseen Monsters	Seizing control of my thoughts and words	
4	The Unseen Monsters	Take time to acknowledge how I feel	
5	What I Miss About HGLD	Things I miss about 'HGLD'	
6	What I Love About HGLD	Things I love about 'HGLD'	
7	What I Learned From HGLD	Braindrops from my loved one	
7	What I Learned From HGLD	Transforming regrets into lifelong learnings	
8	What I Am Grateful to HGLD For	What I am grateful for about _____	

8	What I Am Grateful to HGLD For	Going to bed with gratitude and waking up with love	
9	The One Where....	Creating your own little jar of happy moments	
10	The Most Wonderful Time of the Year (Really?)	Planning my firsts, seconds, and thirds	
10	The Most Wonderful Time of the Year (Really?)	Create your own uplifting playlist	
11	Dipping a Toe in the Pool of the Future	What your loved one wants for you	
11	Dipping a Toe in the Pool of the Future	What I can't and what I can control	
11	Dipping a Toe in the Pool of the Future	Embrace your own words of love, resilience, and strength	
11	Dipping a Toe in the Pool of the Future	Write a letter to your loved one	
11	Dipping a Toe in the Pool of the Future	Go out into nature	
12	Reality Check	Time for a reality check	
13	Making Progress	Holding myself accountable	
14	Borrowing Tractors	Borrowing tractors	

Reviewing these resilience-building exercises now, and perhaps again after a little time has passed, will help you to identify and take some powerful but easy-to-do actions. This opportunity to review your 'Baby Steps' can also show you the progress you are making, over time, in creating your very own new normal, where you know that, despite your loss...

Love Remains

CHAPTER 14:

BORROWING TRACTORS

REMEMBER ME

DAVID HARKINS

Do not shed tears when I have gone but smile instead because I
have lived.
Do not shut your eyes and pray to God that I'll come back but open
your eyes and see all that I have left behind.
I know your heart will be empty because you cannot see me but still
I want you to be full of the love we shared.
You can turn your back on tomorrow and live only for yesterday or
you can be happy for
tomorrow because of what happened between us yesterday.
You can remember me and grieve that I have gone or you can cher-
ish my memory and let it live on.
You can cry and lose yourself, become distraught and turn your back
on the world or you can do what I want — smile, wipe away the tears,
learn to love again and go on.

Before I go, I want to share with you a short story I wrote, inspired by
HGLD, that was published in the internationally best-selling uplifting anthology book *Ignite Possibilities*. I wrote this story at the time
he passed to express my gratitude for the lifetime of love and guidance
he poured into me and the possibilities he unleashed and inspired in me.
I realize how undeniably fortunate I was to have HGLD as my dad and
how his presence has shaped my life. I share this story with you here

to convey with absolute sincerity and from the perspective of personal experience that the memories, experiences, and lessons we learn from our loved ones stay with us to comfort, empower, and inspire us. When we write our story and look back on all we have shared together, all that has made our life better, happier, and uniquely connected because of our special bond with that one person, it offers a healing hug, even while grieving our loss. Immersing myself in writing this story allowed some very timely happy memories to bubble up through my sorrow and gave me the strength to know that I would be okay.

You too have a story, many in fact with your very own *'HGLD.'* They may be about the adventures you shared, the obstacles you overcame together, the growth you sparked in each other, the deep, supporting, and reassuring connection that gave great purpose and meaning to your relationship, or they may be about the *'Braindrops'* they left with you to help you through your life. When you look back on your shared journey of ups, downs, tears, laughter, encouragement, and growth, you too will be left in no doubt whatsoever that the *Love Remains*.

BORROWING TRACTORS

I am the luckiest person I know. Seriously. Unreservedly. Absolutely, toe-tinglingly, lip-smackingly, shamrock tiara-wearingly, blissed-out lucky.

That said, there have been times when I haven't always felt quite so lucky. Times like the many spectacularly failed relationships and the ex who tried to secretly remortgage my house and forged my signature so effectively that he left me in debt up to my eyelashes. Not to mention a whole series of close-shave vehicular near-death experiences, including the car crash that very nearly snuffed out my short and unlived life, which an optimistic person would say are a testament to my instincts and razor-sharp reactions. In fact, I like to believe that the Grim Reaper has gotten so accustomed to me being in his peripheral vision that I have blended into the scenery, and he actually ignores me now! Lucky? Yes! My glass is way more than half full.

I truly thought that I had been through the emotional wringer so many times that I was primed and ready for what was to come. But, on October 16th, 2020 at 12:25 PM, I had the wind knocked out of me in a way I had never experienced. My Dad broke my heart by dying.

To say it had been a heart-wrenching passing would be to understate the stark reality my family found ourselves wading through.

It was a greedy yet invisible quicksand swamp fraught with a Pandora's box of emotions running the gamut from absolute and consuming bone-deep and unconditional love all the way to tortured helplessness and terror via the unfightable undercurrent of acceptance that Dad could not fight the brave fight any longer. He had actually gone.

I was left exhausted and numb as if I had been pushed into a swirling, bottomless, darkly congealed pool of anaesthetic. Every part of my body felt like it was wading through treacle, and the sounds that reached my ears were at best distorted and distant.

Somehow, at the same time, I was also feeling everything and all those conflicting emotions were pouring out of my eyes. I was in sensory overload; a hungry sponge greedily swallowing up every ounce of the pain, turmoil, sadness, abandonment, confusion, denial, and grief that was surrounding me.

Tears were switched to the 'ON' position as if that tap could only be turned off by the immediate return of my adored father. Surely there was something that could reset this? A teeny tiny 'do-over.' I mean, only a moment ago, he was alive! But the ebb and flow of life doesn't work that way; he was gone, and our lives had been forever altered.

HGLD (Handsome God-Like Dad), as I have called him ever since a flash of hero-worshipping inspiration decades ago, had been through an unceasing gladiatorial marathon of health issues over the years, any one of which could cut many to their knees either physically or mentally. Not HGLD. No sirree. He was quite simply special.

If you weren't lucky enough to know him, let me paint you a master-piece. Six-feet tall in his heyday and always standing upright with the tangible and infectious charisma of a true leader. Physically large from a lifetime of enjoying solid Irish man-sized meals (no low-carb, green juice nonsense for him!) but carrying it in a way that only added to his indomitable presence. A full head of professorial hair à la Kirk Douglas, the salt to pepper blend having long ago gracefully given way to salt, much like his diet. Topaz eyes that sparkled endlessly with mischief and a ready smile that echoed and amplified his boyish joie de vivre. Intelligence rolled off and around him like waves eagerly dancing a symphony across an ocean; uncontainable, voracious, probing, bending, advancing, receding, gleefully expanding. Never without a book. Always smartly attired, so much so that he even cut the grass in a crisp white shirt and carefully chosen tie. He was blessed with a fifth appendage, a walking stick that multitasked as an extended finger pointing to any-thing up high or down low that tickled his fancy and caused many a passerby to duck. When he entered a room, the energy surrounding you changed in the most wonderful, palpable, effervescent way. Close your eyes and you can see him.

Above all, this was a man who was the very essence of the belief that ANYTHING IS POSSIBLE. In fact, if you look up 'Possibilities' in the encyclopedia, you will find a picture of him there, positively fizzing with his infectious energy and indefatigable drive.

Dad began his jam-packed life in Wexford, Ireland, the second son of three boys. He lost his mother at the tender age of 2 and was brought up lovingly by his gentle and cultured father, Bill, their devoted house-keeper, Mary Butler, and his Aunty Nellie, the family matriarch who lived next door. Aunty Nellie, a career school teacher who was revered throughout and beyond the town, was a perfect, dignified overseer for the family of three young boys. It was Aunty Nellie who would referee the antics of the boys which would regularly reach fever pitch, and on occasion, blood spilt, generally because of Dad's mischievous nature. As a girl, I loved plying him for stories, listening raptly as he proudly regaled us with many typical boyish scenes, like taking a bite out of the only apple growing on his younger brother's apple tree while it was still on the branch and leaving it to be found by his brother on his daily pilgrimage down the garden with the indisputable evidence of Dad's teeth marks. With glee he would chortle his way through a compendium of memories of youth such as cheating at cards and marbles by distracting his friend's and brother's attention. The latter escapade resulted in him being thrown down the stairs by his rightfully disgruntled siblings! The punishment did nothing to curtail his spark for life and adventure, and I like to imagine that he laughed as he hit every step on his way to the bottom. The resulting broken arm was merely a badge of pride serving to bake in the gleeful memory. Yes, he was indeed special.

How did this boy with a twinkle in his eye turn out? Fast-forward with me to when he first asked my mother out on a date. Another colleague at their office had wanted to court her but was afraid to. So, brazen HGLD asked, originally wishing to inspire his friend by saying, "Ask her, or I will." She said no, which seemed to only increase the value of the prize and did nothing to dissuade his course. Eventually, she agreed on the condition that he would stop asking. Within two years, they were married; a union of devotion like no other which lasted 54 years and to his final breath. Anything is possible!

Dad was a truly loving father to my sister and me. When we were little, he would arrive home in the evening from work and come straight to our rooms to tuck us in for the night where he would quietly retrieve a secretly stashed sweet from his pocket with a conspiratorial wink, instructing us not to tell Mum (sorry Mum!). On Saturday mornings, he would often bring my sister and me to the factory he was General Manager of at the time and would whizz us around the enchanted spaces on an adventure, sweeping through mighty Perspex™ flapped doors on a forklift truck to our squeals of delight. He told us wildly colorful stories, took us on endless magical mystery tours, built forts out of the carpet sweeper, chairs, and a blanket, made us 'egg in a cup' with far more butter than was good for us, but it was so good! He even helped us make daisy crowns and proceeded to regally crown my sister the Queen of Tullyhogue Fairy Fort and me the Princess showing us anything is possible!

This was a man of vision, self-belief, and action who built a hugely successful food processing business based on unused by-products quite
literally thrown away by others working in the same market. He was a
man who became a much-valued consultant who turned businesses
around with his personal blend of grit, vigor, inspiration, philosophy,
psychology, and 20:20 vision for how to turn any problem into a successful solution. He was quite simply unshakeable.

HGLD was a man who could bend reality, long before bending reality
became a trendy buzz phrase. What others saw as *im-possible* he
would charge with his sword of limitless *possibility*.

Always one to make his own luck, he taught me to neither hang back
or hope for luck, nor to admit defeat at life's many inevitable hurdles,
but rather to seize the moment and take action. Dad's words still echo
in my head, "Just make a plan and follow it through." He made moun-
tainous tasks seem like simple 'no-brainers' and, to him, the impossible
just took a little more planning. His light had burned bright; a strong,
vital, stimulating, nourishing, hypnotic, inspiring life force. His gravita-
tional pull was so omnipresent that it had never realistically crossed my
mind that he could be eclipsed. Yet somehow, he was actually gone.
That brilliant light had been quenched, and I found myself shrouded
in shadow — dented, bleeding love, and suddenly doubting my ability
to move forward.

I silently sat watching over him early on the morning of his funeral,
eagerly taking my turn to keep him company before he was forever
removed from our lives. It hit me then, like the proverbial brick. Perhaps
more like a ton of them. HE WAS NOT GONE. He had GONE nowhere.
Yes, his body had valiantly fought its last battle, and, as all knights
eventually do, he had lowered his sword to finally rest. God knows he
deserved to rest. Stationed there, enveloped by the easy chair and
held up by invisible marionette strings, savoring this precious time
with my HGLD, I picked up my laptop, balanced it on my knees, and

started writing. The words, inspired by the life and times of this Titan before me, flowed like a crystal brook, gambolling over the pebbles, navigating their course, freely and abundantly, bubbling over each other onto the page.

It was then I heard his voice as clear in my head as if he was truly speaking out loud, not lying there silently, unsettlingly, and unyieldingly cold to the touch in a box. I realized all his many life lessons and profound yet simple insights were embroidered in the most colorful rainbow of silks into the tapestry of my heart and mind. A waterfall of his braindrops that comforted and advised were stitched into the very fiber of my being.

Sitting there in his still powerful presence, it struck me that I was his legacy. He had not only woven in his pearls of wisdom but had fearlessly walked the talk of 'make your own luck.' He had gallantly opened that same door to me and to all who were blessed to have known him. I was not alone. Neither was I unequipped. His appetite to embrace life was his unwavering gift to me. Mine to keep, grow, adapt, share, enjoy, and take comfort from indefinitely.

Draped in a veil of memories, my mind was full of his zest for living, his stories, and his vast passion for life. One story in particular came bubbling up. It's a story he has told so often that it is tattooed indelibly on my soul. It's an inspirational and unexpected tale about borrowing tractors. After all, we Irish are a nation of farmers.

The story goes something like this… There was a farmer, let's call him Joe, whose tractor had broken down, so he decided to ask his good friend who lived up the road on the next farm if he could borrow his. So, it being a lovely day off, he sets out walking spritely up the road. However, Joe suddenly recalls that he had borrowed some money from his friend a few months ago and hadn't paid it back yet; "He'll never lend me his tractor." Still, Joe walks on. A few minutes later, he remembers that he borrowed his friend's fancy new tools and hadn't given them back; "If he remembers that, I have no chance of borrowing his tractor." Still, Joe pressed onward. As he turns and walks up the path to his friend's house, he sees the man's wife and is reminded of the recent party where he secretly stole a drunken kiss from her; "No damn way will he lend me his tractor." By now, he is full of frustration and 'solid' reasons why he won't get what he wants. Joe knocks angrily on the door and stands waiting, getting more frustrated by the second. His friend opens the door, smiles in greeting at his neighbor, delighted with the visit, and extends his hand in friendship. Joe, enraged and full of negativity, yells at his confused friend, "You can keep your damn tractor," and marches back home, tractorless.

All through my life, any time Dad suspected I was making excuses or chickening out of taking action, all he needed to do was ask me if I was borrowing tractors. This simple story stops me in my tracks to this very day and constantly challenges me to reevaluate what is possible. And it's a story that I've shared with hundreds of people since.

I may not have quite realized it, but I had always been Dad's avid student, drinking heartily from the overflowing font of his knowledge and experience. Watching, listening, learning, assimilating, and embracing all that made Dad so truly electric, so packed full of possibilities. Every lesson was imbibed, stored away, pulled out and used, repurposed, repackaged, fueling my own life, my decisions, my actions. His words, his lessons, his presence were there within me in a way that I just knew and understood with absolute certainty and clarity. His lessons and parables are stored away, and I can still hear his voice so clearly. I can hear the pure honesty and intention. He is with me.

At that moment, I realized it was time to get out of my own way, step out from the shadows of self-doubt and into the golden rays of infinite possibility. I closed the lid on my laptop and leaned back in my chair. I opened my heart, mind, and body to this empowering choice; I felt strong, resilient, focused, lucky. Suddenly, things that I had previously believed to be impossible pipe dreams became not only possible but completely achievable! Instead of borrowing tractors and saying, "I can't do that because...," I ignite my greatest wishes simply by changing my words to "In order to do that, what I need to do is...." Changing my words leads to a truly transformational shift in my beliefs, actions, and feelings.

Since I kissed HGLD's forehead for the last time, I have given myself free rein to accept that I actually have limitless potential and that anything I choose to achieve is possible. It might not be easy or quick but it IS possible. Accepting that fully has liberated me from countless swirling, wasted hours arguing myself out of realizing my dreams or taking action. That, in turn, has lifted my energy and shifted my inner dialogue with ninja-like stealth as I am no longer fighting my self-imposed limitations. I feel lighter. Happier. More me. The real me.

That mind-expanding, life-transforming, boundless potential... *is inside of all of us*. It's a birthright, bestowed in our genetic makeup. It's quietly there, fizzing and tingling like electricity, just waiting to be given permission to use its voice, to spring panther-like into action. The truth is, the only permission we ever need to unleash our limitless potential... *is our own*.

There are no ifs, buts, or can'ts. Now it's all about 'How.' It's a beautiful place to live! In fact, the view is quite simply breathtaking. Why don't you join me? I unreservedly encourage you to step out from any shadows or limiting beliefs holding you back. Know that you do not need anybody's permission but your own. Give it wholeheartedly and unconditionally. Choose to have the life you desire. Choose to know that you are already enough in every way. Bask in the shimmering glow of your very own infinite possibilities.

"The only permission you need to tap into your limitless potential is your own."

TRACY STONE

BABY STEPS

Life flows so much better when we just get out of our own way and allow ourselves to succeed. I challenge you to think about a time when you 'borrowed a tractor.'

Borrowing Tractors

Here's what to do:

1. Think about something you wanted or want to achieve but believe you can't.

2. Write down (yes, actually write or type it down — this action of taking it from your head down onto paper is a game-changer) all the reasons you have for not being able to achieve the thing you wanted. Let's call them 'Limitations.'

3. Now, beside those Limitations, capture what it would actually take to achieve what you want, let's call these the 'Needs.' Check your Needs from the perspective of someone who knows and supports you; would they agree that these are really necessary?

4. Now, beside each of the Needs, drill down a level to identify the Action Steps required to achieve each Need.

5. Finally, realize the truth; if you CHOOSE it and really want it, you can make it happen.

Wants	*Example:* To feel less alone
Limitations	He/she was my everything and now is gone My identity without him/her is unclear My children are grown and have moved away
Needs	Acceptance that my life has altered Willingness to be around others To sometimes do what I don't feel like doing, such as going out or having a chat on the phone To remember the role I play in other people's lives
Action Steps	Give myself permission to accept the fact that my life has altered through my loss of him/her and this is not negotiable Accept that what is negotiable is how I live and what choices I make from now on Do the 'Baby Steps' exercises from Chapter 11 Find someone who needs my help (friend, family member, charity) Have a call or video call with a family member or friend every day Make plans to meet family and friends

Wants			
Limitations			
Needs			
Action Steps			

Now that you have identified any 'tractors' you were borrowing that have been limiting what's possible in your life, and the actions you would need to take to move forward without these limitations.... All that remains is to choose to take the steps to pursue what you want.

You only need your own permission.

As you close this book, it is not the end but just the beginning of a new, resilient, and more contented chapter of your life. The work you have done with the help of the *Baby Steps* will be the cornerstone of your personalized *guide through grief,* providing a gentle, caring space as you build on the comforting foundations of love within you. My wish is that you come to realize that you don't need to let go of the person you love or stop grieving and missing them in order to move forward with life and allow happiness back in. Adjustment to the new path ahead, confidence in yourself, and connection to those you hold dearest in your life and heart will come from a strength and resourcefulness you never even knew existed within you. Be kind and patient with yourself, and know that Love Remains.

I understand the evolving process of grief and the monumental heart and effort it can take to make your way through it. If you need me, the perspective I have gained, or some guidance to help light the way, you can find me here in these pages. I am here for *you.*

Supporting you in your healing and providing a safe space to grow into this next chapter of your life, aided by your own deeply personalized guide, as unique as your relationship with your loved one, has been my privilege. Together we will get through this.

If, while navigating through your unique journey of loss, you want to explore additional galvanizing and comforting *Baby Steps* and expand your personal guide through grief, I have more help available for you. For personal one-to-one support or the digital course that takes you through these and more exercises and bring forth the love that remains, either scan the following QR Code using the camera on your smartphone or reach out to me directly at https://limitlesspotential.co.uk/love-remains.

GLOSSARY

As a student of my own work and processing my own grief, I diligently did each Baby Step in this book myself to foster acceptance, healing, and resilience in my own life. Working my way through the exercises helped me to relive, enjoy, and gain immense contentment and peace of mind from knowing that all I shared with HGLD is mine to keep forever. I wanted to share some of that uplifting and evergreen life force of love with you. Here are some of the things I have learned, grown from, and hold dear to my heart, all courtesy of HGLD.

HGLD's Braindrops

- *If you don't ask, you don't get.* This was never, ever intended from a greedy 'I want more' perspective but from bravery. Dad taught me to stand up and be counted. To always be the first to put my hand up, whether to ask a question, to offer help, or say yes to an opportunity.

- *If you love what you're doing, you'll never work a day in your life.* I'm sure I've heard this one more times than I've had hot dinners. But it's so true. We may not all be in our ideal job at any given time, but this braindrop was about taking accountability for our choices. It was about bravery and finding joy in what we do. It was also about being willing to put in the effort to get from where you are to where you want to be. That's the real differentiator.

- *Are you working hard or hardly working?* Dad was an inexhaustibly hard worker who truly got great happiness from every single day of his working life. He found it very difficult to understand people not wanting to work hard and taught me to embrace the challenge, development, opportunity, pride, and sheer enjoyment to be found through hard work.

- *If a thing's worth doing, it's worth doing well.* He had neither time nor tolerance for shortcuts, being wise enough and long enough in the tooth to know that shortcuts ultimately take longer and generally result in redoing the work, more effort, and frustration. He was a man who took pride in doing something well and, let's just say that the apple didn't fall far from the tree.

- *Don't suffer fools gladly.* Now, this didn't mean he was unkind or intolerant of people. He was, with most people and in the great majority of situations, kind, patient, and caring to a fault. But he was also wily and super fast to read the truth of a situation. HGLD was nobody's fool, he was no martyr, and he absolutely was nobody's sucker.

- *Take a 360-degree view.* Consider any problem from a 360-degree perspective; consider all the angles, all perspectives, even those you don't agree with or want to take into account. This is the way to truly understand the nature of a problem or situation, to get to the root cause, and to gravitate to the best solution. For me, I describe this as the 'Matrix Moment.' That point from the iconic first *Matrix*™ movie when Neo *'gets it.'* To this day, I'm not sure whether this one is a lesson learned, a skill evolved, or whether it's genetically incubated, distilled, and passed down from his grade A, five-star brain DNA. What I am gratefully sure of is that, whatever it is, I've got it, and I exercise it like a ninja.

- *Up there (touching the head) for thinking, down there (pointing to feet) for dancing.* By this, he meant quite simply to engage your brain rather than just step into something without thinking. This would be frequently alternated with...

- *Think it through, then follow it through.* His version of 'measure twice and cut once.' Dad was big on thinking, on truly looking at a situation, and only then taking action. Not to say that he was a ditherer — far from it. His mind, up until the dementia hit in the final few years, was a finely tuned precision machine. But thinking, weighing up the facts and angles, and planning were all as critical to him as the action to follow.

- *Bing, bing, bing.* This was used to great effect to ensure that the following through after the thinking through of any situation was seen as simple, straightforward, and second nature and would go something like this, "Once you have figured out what it is that you need to do, just identify the very first step, then bing, bing, bing!" The implication is that the momentum will carry you if you have planned well.

- *Straight, straight, straight.* These were the critical part of Dad's directions to get anyone from Point A to Point B. In practice, it might have been something like "Go to the crossroads, turn right, take the first left, then straight, straight, straight." I can't even say those words without seeing his right-hand slice vertically and definitely through the air in 90-degree arcs from the elbow to reinforce his point with every 'straight.' It was never meant to be exactly literal, but the intended, brilliant, and inspirational message was that *it's easy.* Believe it's easy, and it will be. And you know what? It works.

- *Never borrow tractors.* Don't 'meet trouble halfway' and don't find ways to talk yourself out of what you know you want or need to do. Talk yourself into taking action, not out of it.

- *Break their arm off.* This was the encouragement that inevitably and immediately accompanied an amped-up twinkle in his eye when we would discuss any opportunity that crossed my path which would result in my development. HGLD was totally on board with regretting doing something rather than regretting not taking the chance. What do you have to lose? Do it. You will figure it out.

- *"Neither a borrower nor a lender be."* This quote from Hamlet, advice issued from Polonius to his son Laertes, was one that HGLD, in practice may not have always followed, but I understood the intention. Dad helped many people out financially over the years, but I also know that he was reluctant to borrow and would avoid that where possible. He vividly and colorfully articulated for us many times the near-heart attack he had at the very beginning of married life to arrive home from work to their tiny flat in Cork city, to find a brand new fridge freezer had suddenly, without either warning or the funds necessary to acquire it, appeared in the kitchen. Mum was thrilled with herself to have bargained with the shop owner and agreed a payment plan. Dad, I'm fairly certain, didn't sleep soundly until it was fully paid off, and he made sure that happened at lightning speed, taking precedence over every expenditure other than their rent. As for the lending part of this particular nugget, he would happily give away his last penny to anyone if he thought they needed it, but he was also aware that once money exchanges hands, in the words of Polonius, as he continued to counsel his son, "For loan oft loses both itself and a friend."

- *If you earn a pound but spend a pound and a penny, that's misery. However, if you earn a pound but spend 99 pennies, that's bliss.* Dad was big on living within our means. Cutting our cloth to suit our means. Earn it before you spend it was the moral and remains sage advice.

- *Never go to sleep on an argument.* Search for the agreement. Pick your battles wisely. Agree to disagree. This was pretty much all the relationship advice Dad would proffer and, as far as he was concerned, it applied to all relationships. I have to admit I fully agree and have found that, while in practice it might not always be easy, palatable, or even possible, it certainly is the aspiration.

What I Love About HGLD

- His twinkling eyes

- How he would crack himself up telling the same jokes or stories over and over

- That he would take my sister and me on 'magical mystery tours'

- How he would let me snuggle up with him in the big swivel chair to watch our favorite programs on TV

- Christmas dinner was an extravaganza of which he was King

- That he loved everything about Christmas and embraced it like a child; festive movies, music, Christmas trees in every room, lights, and decorations everywhere

- How he loved animals and they loved him

- The wondrous, far-fetched yet enthralling stories he would spin for us as children

- His natural and unconquerable positive 'can-do' attitude and habits

- His amazing intelligence both learned from the subject matter and human behavior

- His love of beautiful music

- How he would conduct music as he drove

- His ability to make up ridiculous and hilarious words to songs when he didn't know what they were

- His boarding school stories of escapades with friends like raiding the pantry in the dark of night to pilfer the butter

- How he would enthusiastically deliver a huge and forceful wave at almost every person he drove past, calling each unknown and unmet friend 'John-Joe' and every woman 'Mary.'

- How he would stick his tongue out the side of his mouth when he concentrated

- How he would so carefully select his shirt, tie, and cardigan each day and wear them with pizzazz and flair

- When he walked into a room, you knew he was there

- He was full of the childish mischief of a young boy

- He loved living near the sea

- That he was truly loved by so many

- His love of rum and raisin ice cream

- How when he ate something he really loved, he wouldn't speak and his eyes would roll up in his head from sheer pleasure

- That he built a family he loved dearly after losing his own parents while still young

- He helped more people than I will ever know out of their difficulty

- Despite being a large man, women were putty in his hands, but...

- He only had eyes for Mum

- He shared more lessons in life with us than the Bible

- That I have inherited many of his traits and characteristics

Things I'm Grateful to HGLD for

- The creative magic he would sprinkle, when he could, into our childhood through mythical, mystical, and often madcap stories and adventures that would enthrall us, where anything could happen. There were no rules his imagination would run riot, whipping us up with it along the way.

- How he would come straight to our bedrooms to tuck us in at night when he returned from work, usually with a sweet treat hidden in his pocket.

- That he loved spending time with us and was entirely good with us snuggling up to his large and comforting frame as he would watch TV from his favorite armchair.

- The amazing roast dinner he would enjoy cooking every Sunday with plenty of succulent tender but well-done beef and no shortage of beautifully crisp roast potatoes and lashings of gravy. Hmmmmmm.

- The extravaganza of blockbuster proportions when he made the roast turkey dinner every Christmas and how he would pull out all the stops to ensure we all had what we wanted, and lashings of it.

- How he made Christmas so special for us all. Some years he dressed up as Santa Claus to hand out gifts to the children at the factory Christmas party. Every Christmas morning, he would lock the living room door where the tree and presents were (not fair!) while he got the meal of epic proportions underway so he could be ready with his prized old-style — though brand new back then in the 1970s — cine camera in hand to capture every squeal of

delight as his two little princesses flittered open their gifts.

- The love, adoration, and security he devoted to Mum. Caring for her was undoubtedly his purpose for breathing.

- The beautiful homes and security he worked hard to provide for Mum and us girls.

- The lessons he taught us that have helped my sister and me along the path of our own lives.

- That he was a tireless mentor to anyone who showed signs of promise, passion, or potential. In my case, I knew that he would never, ever say no if I came to him for advice or to just mull something over. He was giving of his time, knowledge, and his ear.

- That he cared enough to deeply instill in us some key lessons that he firmly believed would benefit us. And they did. And they still do.

- That he had faith in me and what I was capable of, even when I didn't.

- His sincerity and generosity which were bone-deep.

- His sense of humor which provided great balance to all the times of pressure.

- His infectious 'can-do' attitude. No mountain was ever too high, no problem too great, no situation impossible.

- The memories I get to keep forever of all our times together, lessons shared, love nurtured. Forever mine to hold, glean comfort from, use, reuse, develop further, and share onward with others.

Things I miss about HGLD

- Sitting together in Dad's favorite restaurant in Windsor enjoying a burger, fried onion strings, banter-filled chat, and our undeniable closeness while Mum enjoyed a look around the shops.

- Fishing with him on Lough Corrib in the west of Ireland when I was a child, helping him prep and push his little blue fiberglass boat out into the water, and pretty much always coming back empty-handed but happy.

- Sharing our libraries of books, both of us relishing the frivolous fiction that would bring dashing characters like Alex Cross and Jack Reacher leaping off the page.

- Accompanying him as a young girl on regular journeys from Wexford to Dublin, using that time strategically to pester him with endless questions about his childhood.

- How he would laugh at his own incredibly silly jokes, which were rarely original or actually all that funny, but he would mine them for every minuscule grain of golden giggle dust.

- How, even when tired, he would happily join me in the car to buy a pint of milk, just for the opportunity for a chat, and from fear he would miss out on any excitement.

- How he would suit up with his coat zipped, buttons buttoned, snappers snapped, from top to toe, hat pulled snugly down over his ears, scarf always matching his tie which was folded neatly around his neck and down his chest, gloves on, shoes shined, walking stick in hand, and book under his arm, standing by the front door 20 minutes before we ever had to leave the house telling us all we were going to be late.

- Seeing him mowing the lawn on his ride-on mower, loving the freedom and mobility that his legs had long since denied him. Almost as good as being a getaway driver from a bank heist in a movie!

- How he would love watching and feeding all the local birds or 'birdeens' as my Nana (Mum's Mum) would call the teeny-weeny little ones. This peaceful and heart-expanding activity would always make him feel close to Nana, who he adored.

- Seeing him enjoy a charred yet juicy inside steak with a 'mess' of fried onions or his favorite takeaway fried chicken when he would have extended holidays with me in England. Seriously, nobody could imagine the abstract pleasure that he got from the £4.50 meal. I don't think a Rolls Royce would have made him any happier.

- How he would make a 'mud pie' on his plate out of any meal which involved mashed potatoes, gravy, or a sauce of any kind. He would do this for my sister and me when we were little in a somewhat misguided effort to get us to eat up whatever vegetable we were artfully dodging.

- His constant encouragement, which would propel me forward in my career, buoyed up by the belief he instilled in me that I could achieve anything.

- When my sister and I were little, he could make anything mundane feel like an adventure.

- How when either my sister or I was being gently reprimanded, he would refer to us as 'Luvvie.'

- The heady scent of his Fahrenheit aftershave, always liberally applied then lingering and wafting around him like a heavenly cloud.

- His inexhaustible positivity.

- His natural ability to rise above adversity of any shape, kind, or form.

- Seeing how fast his brain worked. It was like watching a sped-up ballet.

- His voice. Though I can hear that at any time I choose.

In sharing my story and all the things I have learned from my beloved HGLD, my wholehearted wish is for you to know that *you are amazing*. You are *wiser* and *more courageous* than you realize. You matter. You have so much to share with others to enhance their lives. All you will ever need to tap into your unshakeable inner strength is already baked into your DNA. Everything you need is there within you, helping, guiding, protecting, caring for you, and paving the way ahead with the love that remains.

NOTES PAGES

There may be times when you feel a little overwhelmed by your thoughts or responsibilities, and they end up going around in circles fighting for attention in your mind, leaving you stressed, bewildered, or stuck. Sometimes you just need to capture your thoughts, so you don't lose them, allowing you time to step away from them until you decide to revisit and deal with that thought another day.

We all need a little time and space every now and then to allow our thoughts to take shape, to fully form, and to put them into a more 'doable' context or to save them to enjoy later.

There's a very simple approach that works brilliantly in giving you this necessary breathing space for your thoughts. *Write them down.*

On a piece of paper, in a journal, or here in the 'Notes' pages of this book, write down everything you are worried about, whether it's the thoughts you have about the person you are grieving or the tasks, obligations, and things going on in your life that are consuming your thoughts and your energy.

When you write down your thoughts, something almost magical happens. Your mind calms and reorganizes. As your feelings and emotions come to the surface and become clearer, the process of writing them down adds perspective, logic, and light to the situation.

It's also helpful to write down your happy, joy-filled, empowering reflections.

Use the space created here to capture your thoughts. Allow yourself the benefit of clearing your mind a little to pave the way for acceptance, healing, decision-making, and taking action.

What's on my mind

What I need to do and why I need to do it

Happy thoughts

What I am grateful for

RESOURCES

Organizations USA

- https://forums.grieving.com/
- https://www.griefincommon.com/
- https://www.griefanonymous.com/facebook-groups/

Organizations Canada

- https://www.chpca.ca/
- https://ofsa.org/grief_support_resources
- https://www.mygrief.ca/

Organizations UK

- https://www.thegoodgrieftrust.org/our-library/
- https://www.cruse.org.uk/about-cruse/publications/
  recommended-books
- https://www.tcf.org.uk/content/r-reading-list/
- https://www.mariecurie.org.uk/
- https://www.supportline.org.uk/problems/bereavement/
- https://www.mentalhealth.org.uk/coronavirus/
  change-loss-and-bereavement
- https://www.nhs.uk/
- https://www.mind.org.uk/

Organizations UK & Ireland

- https://www.samaritans.org/

Organizations Ireland

- https://www.alzint.org/member/alzheimer-society-of-ireland/
- http://www.aftering.com/
- https://hospicefoundation.ie/our-supports-services/
  bereavement-loss-hub/bereavement-support-line/
- https://www.bethany.ie/

Poems

- "Reflections" by Traci Harrell, Traci@ItsAllBiggerThanMe.com,
  www.ItsAllBiggerThanMe.com
- "Requiescat in Pace" by Libbie C. Baer, https://poets.org/poem/
  requiescat-pace
- "Grief in me'"by JB Owen, best-selling author, publisher, mom of
  four
- "Time Is Kind' by Dr Raolee, educator, author, speaker, and
  sickle cell warrior, Raolee21@gmail.com, www.dr10k.com
- "The Window" by Rumi https://melancholyheart.wordpress.
  com/2012/06/23/the-window/
- "A Robin Red" by Georgina Murdoch-Stone
- "If" by Rudyard Kipling, https://poets.org/poem/if
- "That Man is a Success" by Robert Louis Stevenson, https://
  www.quotes.net/quote/1785
- "In Lieu of Flowers" by Shawna Lemay, from The Flower Can
  Always Be Changing, Palimpsest Press, 2018
- "Found You" by Sheryl Bates, https://www.familyfriendpoems.
  com/poem/found-you
- "It's a Long Way" by William Stanley Braithwaite, https://poets.
  org/poem/its-long-way
- "The Jigsaw" by Doesitsay
- "Remember Me" by David Harkins, https://www.griefandsympa-
  thy.com/funeral-poem-remember-me.html

Takotsubo Syndrome

- https://www.bhf.org.uk/informationsupport/
  heart-matters-magazine/medical/what-is-takotsubo-syndrome
- https://www.nhs.uk/conditions/cardiomyopathy/
- https://www.mayoclinic.org/diseases-conditions/
  broken-heart-syndrome/symptoms-causes/syc-20354617#:~:-
  text=Broken%20heart%20syndrome%20is%20
  a,cardiomyopathy%20or%20apical%20ballooning%20
  syndrome
- https://www.health.harvard.edu/heart-health/
  takotsubo-cardiomyopathy-broken-heart-syndrome

Hormones and grief

- https://www.henryford.com/blog/2018/06/how-coping-with-
  grief-can-affect-your-brain#:~:text=When%20you're%20
  grieving%2C%20a,brain%20function%20takes%20a%20hit
- https://neurosciencenews.com/grief-neuroendocrine-16771/
- https://medicalxpress.com/news/2021-03-grief-rewires-brain-
  affect-healthand.html
- https://www.heart.org/en/news/2021/03/10/how-grief-rewires-
  the-brain-and-can-affect-health-and-what-to-do-about-it

Gratitude

- https://www.uclahealth.org/marc/default.cfm
- https://www.focusforhealth.org/
  gratitude-our-bodies-natural-anti-depressant/
- https://positivepsychology.com/neuroscience-of-gratitude/
- https://gratefulness.org/brother-david/about-brother-david/
- https://www.tandfonline.com/doi/full/10.1080/17439760.2018.14
  24924?scroll=top&needAccess=true

Spoon Theory

- Created by Christine Miserandino www.butyoudontlooksick. com/the_spoon_theory

Other

- Esther Rantzen: Living With Grief, Channel 5 tv UK
- https://www.nytimes.com/2021/04/22/well/what-happens-in-the-body-during-grief.html
- https://www.health.harvard.edu/mind-and-mood/how-to-overcome-griefs-health-damaging-effects
- https://www.webmd.com/mental-health/ss/slideshow-grief-health-effects
- https://www.apa.org/monitor/2020/06/covid-grieving-life#

Contributors

- Charlene Ray MSW, LICSW Grief Counselor, www.charleneray. com, soulwisdomguide@gmail.com
- Pat Labez, best-selling author, actor, producer, speaker, advocate, www.ThirdActEncore.com
- Esther Keene
- Margaret Stone
- Georgina Murdoch-Stone
- Ciara Jackson

ABOUT THE AUTHOR

Tracy Stone is a renowned clinical hypnotherapist, advanced RTT® therapist, transformational coach and best-selling author originally from Wexford, Ireland, and now based in Berkshire, UK.

Before becoming a clinical hypnotherapist, Tracy spent 32 years in some of the world's largest and most prestigious global businesses helping senior management teams maximize their strengths and eliminate major process issues. From New York to Sydney, she built a phenomenal reputation as a world-class problem solver and 'transformation whisperer.' Her many awards are testament to her ability to make concrete and significant changes to the thousands who have joined her much acclaimed workshops, trainings, and coaching events.

Tracy has taken those years of experience in identifying the true root cause of problems and uncovering solutions that provide results and now uses her finely tuned skills to make spectacular and lasting transformational shifts in her client's personal lives through her courses, coaching, and hypnotherapy.

"Whether it means resolving the burdens held onto from childhood or the doubts which have crept into the mind along life's trials, I work with my clients to help them quickly and permanently let go of what's holding them back and liberate themselves to live the life they want."

In October 2020, Tracy's father died in the midst of the COVID-19 pandemic. The loss of such a pivotal character in her life encouraged her to share through *Love Remains* her experience of grief along with the experiences of a few special people and a carefully curated selection of tools or exercises to help others to manage their journey through grief.

If you are ready to set down the baggage and overcome the limitations that hold you back in life... Tracy is ready to help you make it happen.

Made in United States
North Haven, CT
06 June 2022

19945327R00143